Back to Basics: Personal Finance

by Eric Tyson, MBA

WILEY

Publisher's Acknowledgments

Editorial Project Manager:
Victoria M. Adang

Senior Acquisitions Editor:
Tracy Boggier

Production Editor: Antony Sami

Cover Images: (magnifying glass)
© AVicons / Getty Images, (house)
© Agaten / Getty Images, (pot of gold)
© jamtoons / Getty Images

Cover Design: Wiley

Back to Basics: Personal Finance

Published by John Wiley & Sons, Inc.
111 River St.
Hoboken, NJ 07030-5774
http://www.wiley.com

Contents

1 Improving Your Financial Literacy...............1

Talking Money at Home 3

Hurdles to Financial Success. 5

2 Measuring Your Financial Health...............11

Common Money Mistakes 12

Determine Your Financial Net Worth. 16

Bad Debt versus Good Debt 21

Analyze Your Savings. 27

Assess Your Insurance Savvy 30

3 Establishing Goals...........................33

A Definition of Wealth 34

Savings Goals 38

Emergency Reserves. 42

Saving to Buy a Home or Business 44

Educational Expenses 45

Big Purchases. 46

4 Spending Habits.............................49

Overspending 50

Analyze Your Spending. 57

5 Credit Scores and Reports 67

Credit Data 67

Obtaining Your Credit Reports and Score 70

Improving Your Credit Reports and Score. 72

Correcting Credit Report Errors 74

6 Retirement..................................77

How Much You Need for Retirement. 78

Tax Advantages 81

Retirement Building Blocks 82

Estimate Your Retirement Savings 89

Make Up for Lost Time 91

7 Reducing Your Spending 95

Keys to Successful Spending. 96

Budget to Boost Your Savings 100

Reduce Your Spending 102

8 Debt. 121

Using Savings to Reduce Your Consumer Debt 122

Decreasing Debt When You Lack Savings 127

Credit Counseling Agencies 134

Stopping the Spending Cycle. 139

9 Filing Bankruptcy 145

Bankruptcy Benefits 146

Bankruptcy Drawbacks 147

Bankruptcy Laws 149

Chapter 7 and Chapter 13 Bankruptcy. 152

Seeking Bankruptcy Advice 153

10 Taxes 155

The Taxes You Pay 155

Employment Income Taxes 161

Deductions 164

Education Tax Breaks 176

11 Insurance 179

Basics of Buying Insurance 180

Insurance Problems 193

12 Technology and Your Money 203

Digital Pros and Cons 204

Accomplishing Money Tasks on Your Digital Device . 211

1

Improving Your Financial Literacy

In recent years, a continuing stream of studies has indicated that Americans are by and large financially illiterate. The vast majority of survey respondents have "failing" scores — meaning that they answered less than 60 percent of the questions correctly.

I know from my many years of work previously as a personal financial counselor and now as a writer that many people have significant gaps in their personal financial knowledge. Though more folks have greater access today to more information than in prior generations, the financial world has grown more complicated, and there are more choices, and pitfalls, than ever before.

Unfortunately, most Americans don't know how to manage their personal finances because they were never taught how to do so. Their parents may have avoided discussing money in front of them, and most high schools and colleges lack courses that teach this vital, lifelong-needed skill.

Some people are fortunate enough to learn the financial keys to success at home, from knowledgeable friends, and from the best expert-written books like this one. Others either never discover important personal finance concepts, or they learn them the hard way — by making lots of costly mistakes. People who lack knowledge make more mistakes, and the more financial errors you commit, the more money passes through your hands and out of your life. In addition to the enormous financial costs, you experience the emotional toll of not feeling in control of your finances. Increased stress and anxiety go hand in hand with not mastering your money.

This chapter examines where people learn about finances and helps you decide whether your current knowledge is helping you or holding you back. You can find out how to improve your financial literacy and take responsibility for your finances, putting you in charge and reducing your anxiety about money.

_____

_____

_____

Talking Money at Home

In many families, money is a taboo subject — parents don't level with their kids about the limitations, realities, and details of their budgets. Some parents believe that dealing with money is an adult issue and that children should be insulated from it so they can enjoy being kids. In many families, kids hear about money *only* when disagreements and financial crises arise. Thus begins the harmful cycle of children having negative associations with money and financial management.

In other cases, parents with the best of intentions pass on their bad money-management habits. You may have learned from a parent, for example, to buy things to cheer yourself up. Or you may have witnessed a family member chasing get-rich-quick business and investment ideas. In the area of personal finance, as in any other area, poor family advice and modeling can be problematic.

Think about where your parents learned about money management and then consider whether they had the time, energy, or inclination to research choices before making their decisions. For example, if they didn't do enough research or

_____

_____

_____

had faulty information, your parents may mistakenly have thought that banks were the best places for investing money or that buying stocks was like going to Las Vegas.

In still other cases, the parents have the right approach, but the kids do the opposite out of rebellion. For example, if your parents spent money carefully and thoughtfully and often made you feel denied, you may tend to do the opposite, buying yourself gifts the moment any extra money comes your way.

Although you can't change what the educational system and your parents did or didn't teach you about personal finances, you now have the ability to find out what you need to know to manage your finances.

If you have children of your own, don't underestimate their potential or send them out into the world without the skills they need to be productive and happy adults. Buy them some good financial books when they head off to college or begin their first job.

Hurdles to Financial Success

Perhaps you know that you should live within your means, buy and hold sound investments for the long term, and secure proper insurance coverage; however, you can't bring yourself to do these things. Everyone knows how difficult it is to break habits that have been practiced for many years. The temptation to spend money lurks everywhere you turn.

Maybe you felt deprived by your tightwad parents as a youngster, or maybe you're bored with life and you like the adventure of buying new things. If only you could hit it big on one or two investments, you think, you could get rich quick and do what you really want with your life. As for disasters and catastrophes, well, those things happen to other people, not to you. Besides, you'll probably have advance warning of pending problems, so you can prepare accordingly, right?

Your emotions and temptations can get the better of you. Certainly, part of successfully managing your finances involves coming to terms with your shortcomings and the consequences of your behaviors. If you don't, you may end up enslaved to a dead-end job so you can keep feeding your spending addiction. Or you may spend more time with your investments than you do with your family and friends. Or unexpected events may leave you reeling financially; disasters and catastrophes can happen to anyone at any time.

What (or who) is holding you back

A variety of personal and emotional hurdles can get in the way of making the best financial moves. A lack of financial knowledge (which stems from a lack of personal financial education) can stand in the way of making good decisions.

Some people get caught in the psychological trap of blaming something else for their financial problems. For example, some people believe that adult problems can be traced back to childhood and how they were raised.

I don't want to disregard the negative impact particular backgrounds can have on some people's tendency to make the wrong choices. Exploring your personal history can certainly yield clues to what makes you tick. That said, adults make choices and engage in behaviors that affect themselves as well as others. They shouldn't blame their parents for their own inability to plan for their financial futures, live within their means, and make sound investments.

_____

_____

_____

Some people also tend to blame their financial shortcomings on not earning more income. Such people believe that if only they earned more, their financial (and personal) problems would melt away. However, achieving financial success — and more important, personal happiness — has virtually nothing to do with how much income a person makes but rather with what she makes of what she has. I know financially wealthy people who are emotionally poor even though they have all the material goods they want. Likewise, I know people who are quite happy, content, and emotionally wealthy even though they're struggling financially.

Americans — even those who have not had an "easy" life — ought to be able to come up with numerous things to be happy about and grateful for: a family who loves them; friends who laugh at their stupid jokes; the freedom to catch a movie or play or to read a good book; or a great singing voice, a good sense of humor, or a full head of hair.

Developing good financial habits

After you understand the basic concepts and know where to buy the best financial products when you need them, you'll soon see that managing personal finances well is not much more difficult than other things you do regularly, like tying your shoelaces and getting to work each day.

Regardless of your income, you can make your dollars stretch farther if you practice good financial habits and avoid mistakes. In fact, the lower your income, the more important it is that you make the most of your income and savings (because you don't have the luxury of falling back on your next big paycheck to bail you out).

More and more industries are subject to global competition, so you need to be on your financial toes now more than ever. Job security is waning; layoffs and retraining for new jobs are increasing.

Odds are increasing that you work for an employer that has you save toward your own retirement instead of providing a pension for you. Not only do you need to save the money, you must also decide how to invest it. Chapter 6 can help you get a handle on investing in retirement accounts.

Personal finance involves much more than managing and investing money. It also includes making all the pieces of your financial life fit together; it means lifting yourself out of financial illiteracy. Like planning a vacation, managing your personal finances means forming a plan for making the best use of your limited time and dollars.

_____

_____

_____

Intelligent personal financial strategies have little to do with your gender, ethnicity, or marital status. All people need to manage their finances wisely. Some aspects of financial management become more or less important at different points in your life, but for the most part, the principles remain the same for everyone.

Knowing the right answers isn't enough. You have to practice good financial habits just as you practice other good habits, such as brushing your teeth or eating a healthy diet and getting some exercise. Don't be overwhelmed. As you read this book, make a short list of your financial marching orders and then start working away.

What you do with your money is a personal and confidential matter. In this book, I try to provide guidance that can keep you in sound financial health. You don't have to take it all — pick what works best for you and understand the pros and cons of your options. But from this day forward, please don't make the easily avoidable mistakes or overlook the sound strategies that I discuss throughout this book.

Throughout your journey, I hope to challenge and even change the way you think about money and about making important personal financial decisions.

_____

_____

_____

2

Measuring Your
Financial Health

How financially healthy are you? When was the last time you reviewed your overall financial situation, including analyzing your spending, savings, future goals, and insurance? If you're like most people, either you've never done this exercise or you did so too long ago.

This chapter guides you through a *financial physical* to help you detect problems with your current financial health. But don't dwell on your problems. View them for what they are — opportunities to improve your financial situation. In fact, the more areas you can identify that stand to benefit from improvement, the greater the potential you may have to build real wealth and accomplish your financial and personal goals.

Common Money Mistakes

Financial problems are best detected early. Here are the common personal financial problems I've seen in my work as a financial counselor:

- **Not planning:** Most of us procrastinate. That's why we have deadlines (like April 15) — and deadline extensions (need another six months to get that tax return done?). Unfortunately, you may have no explicit deadlines with your personal finances. You can allow your credit card debt to accumulate, or you can leave your savings sitting in lousy investments for years. You can pay higher taxes, leave gaps in your retirement and insurance coverage, and overpay for financial products. Of course, planning your finances isn't as much fun as planning a vacation, but doing the former can help you take more of the latter.

- **Overspending:** Simple arithmetic helps you determine that savings is the difference between what you earn and what you spend (assuming that you're not spending more than you're earning). To increase your savings, you either have to work more, increase your earning power through education or job advancement, get to know a wealthy family who wants to leave its fortune to you, or spend less. For most people, especially over the short-term, the thrifty approach is the key to building savings and wealth.

- **Buying with consumer credit:** Even with the benefit of today's low interest rates, carrying a balance month-to-month on your credit card or buying a car on credit means that even more of your future earnings are going to be earmarked for debt repayment. Buying on credit encourages you to spend more than you can really afford.

- **Delaying saving for retirement:** Most folks say that they want to retire by their mid-60s or sooner. But to accomplish this goal, they need to save a reasonable chunk (around 10 percent) of their incomes starting sooner rather than later. The longer you wait to start saving for retirement, the harder reaching your goal will be. And you'll pay much more in taxes if you don't take advantage of the tax benefits of investing through particular retirement accounts.

_____

_____

_____

- **Falling prey to financial sales pitches:** Steer clear of people who pressure you to make decisions, promise you high investment returns, and lack the proper training and experience to help you. Great deals that can't wait for a little reflection or a second opinion are often disasters waiting to happen.

- **Not doing your homework:** To get the best deal, shop around, read reviews, and get advice from objective third parties. You also need to check references and track records so you don't hire incompetent, self-serving, or fraudulent financial advisors.

- **Making decisions based on emotion:** You're most vulnerable to making the wrong moves financially after a major life change or when you feel pressure. Maybe your investments plunged in value. Or perhaps a recent divorce has you fearing that you won't be able to afford to retire when you planned, so you pour thousands of dollars into some newfangled financial product. Take your time and keep your emotions out of the picture.

- **Not separating the wheat from the chaff:** In any field in which you're not an expert, you run the danger of following the advice of someone you think is an expert but really isn't. You are the person who is best able to manage your personal finances. Educate and trust yourself!

- **Exposing yourself to catastrophic risk:** You're vulnerable if you and your family don't have insurance to pay for financially devastating losses. People without a savings reserve and a support network can end up homeless. Many people lack sufficient insurance coverage to replace their income. Don't wait for a tragedy to strike to find out whether you have the right insurance coverage.

- **Focusing too much on money:** Placing too much emphasis on making and saving money can warp your perspective on what's important in life. Money is not the first — or even second — priority in happy people's lives. Your health, relationships with family and friends, career satisfaction, and fulfilling interests are more significant.

Money problems can be fixed over time with changes in your behavior. That's what the rest of this book is all about.

_____

_____

_____

Determine Your Financial Net Worth

Your financial net worth is an important barometer of your monetary health. Your net worth indicates your capacity to accomplish major financial goals, such as buying a home, retiring, and withstanding unexpected expenses or loss of income.

Your *net worth* is your financial assets minus your financial liabilities:

Financial Assets – Financial Liabilities = Net Worth

The following sections explain how to determine those numbers.

Adding up your financial assets

A *financial asset* is real money or an investment you can convert into your favorite currency that you can use to buy things now or in the future. Financial assets generally include the money you have in bank accounts, stocks, bonds, mutual funds, and exchange-traded funds. Money that you have in retirement accounts (including those with your employer) and the value of any businesses or real estate that you own are also counted.

I generally recommend that you exclude your personal residence when figuring your financial assets. Include your home only if you expect to sell it someday or otherwise live off the money you now have tied up in it. If you plan on eventually tapping into the *equity* (the difference between the market value and any debt owed on the property), add that portion of the equity that you expect to use to your list of assets.

Assets can also include your future expected Social Security benefits and pension payments (if your employer has such a plan). These assets are usually quoted in dollars per month rather than as a lump sum value. Table 2-1 shows how to account for these monthly benefits when tallying your financial assets.

Consumer items — such as your car, clothing, smartphone, and so forth — do *not* count as financial assets. Adding these things to your assets makes your assets *look* larger (and some financial software and publications encourage you to list these items as assets), but you can't live off them unless you sell them.

Account	Value
Savings and investment accounts (including retirement accounts):	
Example: Bank savings account	$5,000
_____	$_____
_____	$_____
_____	$_____
_____	$_____
_____	$_____
_____	$_____
Subtotal =	$_____
Benefits earned that pay a monthly retirement income:	
Employer's pensions	$_____ / month
Social Security	$_____ / month
	× 240*
Subtotal =	$_____
Total Financial Assets (add the two subtotals) =	$_____

Table 2-1: *Your Financial Assets*

[1.]*To convert benefits that will be paid to you monthly into a total dollar amount, and for purposes of simplification, assume that you will spend 20 years in retirement. Inflation may reduce the value of your employer's pension if it doesn't contain a cost-of-living increase each year in the same way that Social Security does. Don't sweat this now — you can take care of that concern in the section on retirement planning in Chapter 3.*

Subtracting your financial liabilities

To arrive at your financial net worth, you must subtract your *financial liabilities* from your assets. Liabilities include loans and debts outstanding, such as credit card and auto loan debts. When figuring your liabilities, include money you borrowed from family and friends (unless you're not expected to pay it back).

Include mortgage debt on your home as a liability *only* if you include the value of your home in your asset list. Be sure to also include debt owed on other real estate — no matter what (because you count the value of investment real estate as an asset).

Crunching your numbers

Table 2-1 provides a place for you to figure your financial assets. *Note:* See Table 4-1 in Chapter 4 to estimate your Social Security benefits.

Now comes the potentially depressing part — figuring out your debts and loans in Table 2-2.

Now you can subtract your liabilities from your assets to figure your net worth in Table 2-3.

_____

_____

_____

Loan	Balance
Example: U Bank Credit Card	$4,000
_____	$_____
_____	$_____
_____	$_____
_____	$_____
_____	$_____
_____	$_____
Total Financial Liabilities =	$_____

Table 2-2: *Your Financial Liabilities*

Find	Write It Here
Total Financial Assets (from Table 2-1)	$_____
Total Financial Liabilities (from Table 2-2)	– $_____
Net Worth =	$_____

Table 2-3: *Your Net Worth*

Interpreting your net worth results

Your net worth is important and useful only to you and your unique situation and goals. What seems like a lot of money to a person with a simple lifestyle may seem like a pittance to a person with high expectations and a desire for an opulent lifestyle.

_____

_____

_____

In Chapter 3, you can crunch numbers to determine your financial status more precisely for goals such as retirement planning. In the meantime, if your net worth (excluding expected monthly retirement benefits such as those from Social Security and pensions) is negative or less than half of your annual income, take notice. If you're in your 20s and you're just starting to work, a low net worth is less concerning and not unusual. Focus on turning this number positive over the next several years. However, if you're in your 30s or older, consider this a wake-up call to aggressively address your financial situation.

Getting rid of your debts — the highest-interest rate ones first — is the most important thing. Then you want to build a safety reserve equal to three to six months of living expenses. Your overall plan should involve getting out of debt, reducing your spending, and developing tax-wise ways to save and invest your future earnings.

Bad Debt versus Good Debt

Usually, you borrow money because you don't have enough to buy something you want or need — like a college education. A four-year college education can easily cost $100,000,

$150,000, $200,000, or more. Not too many people have that kind of spare cash. So borrowing money to finance part of that cost enables you to buy the education.

How about a new car? A trip to your local car dealer shows you that a new vehicle will set you back $20,000+. Although more people may have the money to pay for that than, say, the college education, what if you don't? Should you finance the car the way you finance the education?

The auto dealers and bankers who are eager to make you an auto loan say that you deserve and can afford to drive a nice new car, and they tell you to borrow away. I say, "No!" Why do I disagree with the auto dealers and lenders? For starters, I'm not trying to sell you a car or loan from which I derive a profit. More important, there's a *big* difference between borrowing for something that represents a long-term investment and borrowing for short-term consumption.

Consuming your way to bad debt

Bad debt refers to debt incurred for consumption because such debt is harmful to your long-term financial health.

You'll be able to take many more vacations during your lifetime if you save the cash in advance. If you get into the habit of borrowing and paying all the associated interest for vacations, cars, clothing, and other consumer items, you'll spend more of your future income paying back the debt and interest, leaving you with less money for your other goals.

The relatively high interest rates that banks and other lenders charge for bad (consumer) debt is one of the reasons you're less able to save money when using such debt. Not only does money borrowed through credit cards, auto loans, and other types of consumer loans carry a relatively high interest rate, but it also isn't tax deductible.

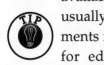

I'm not saying that you should never borrow money and that all debt is bad. Good debt, such as that used to buy real estate and small businesses, is generally available at lower interest rates than bad debt and is usually tax deductible. If well managed, these investments may also increase in value. Borrowing to pay for educational expenses can also make sense. Education is generally a good long-term investment because it can increase your earning potential. And student loan interest is tax deductible, subject to certain limitations (see Chapter 10).

Recognizing bad debt overload

Calculating how much debt you have relative to your annual income is a useful way to size up your debt load. Ignore, for now, good debt — the loans you may owe on real estate, a business, an education, and so on (I cover that in the next section). I'm focusing on bad debt, the higher-interest debt used to buy items that depreciate in value.

To calculate your bad debt danger ratio, divide your bad debt by your annual income:

$$\frac{\text{bad debt}}{\text{annual income}} = \text{bad debt danger ratio}$$

For example, suppose you earn $40,000 per year. Between your credit cards and an auto loan, you have $20,000 of debt. In this case, your bad debt represents 50 percent of your annual income.

The financially healthy amount of bad debt is zero. While enjoying the convenience of credit cards, *never* buy anything with your card that you can't afford to pay off in full when the bill comes at the end of the month.

When your bad debt danger ratio starts to push beyond 25 percent, it can spell real trouble. Such high levels of high-interest consumer debt on credit cards and auto loans grow like cancer. The growth of the debt can snowball and get out of control unless something significant intervenes. If you have consumer debt beyond 25 percent of your annual income, see Chapter 7 to find out how to get out of debt.

How much good debt is acceptable? The answer varies. The key question is: Are you able to save sufficiently to accomplish your goals? In the "Analyze Your Savings" section later in this chapter, I help you figure out how much you're actually saving, and in Chapter 3, I help you determine how much you need to save to accomplish your goals.

Borrow money only for investments (good debt) — for purchasing things that retain and hopefully increase in value over the long term, such as an education, real estate, or your own business. Don't borrow money for consumption (bad debt) — for spending on things that decrease in value and eventually become financially worthless, such as cars, clothing, vacations, and so on.

Assessing good debt

You can get too much of a good thing, including good debt! When you incur debt for investment purposes — to buy real estate, for small business, even your education — you hope to see a positive return on your invested dollars.

But some real estate investments don't work out. Some small businesses crash and burn, and some educational degrees and programs don't help in the way that some people hope they will.

There's no magic formula for determining when you have too much "good debt." In extreme cases, I've seen entrepreneurs, for example, borrow up to their eyeballs to get a business off the ground. Sometimes this works, and they end up financially rewarded, but in most cases, it doesn't.

Here are three important questions to ponder and discuss with your loved ones about the seemingly "good debt" you're taking on:

- Are you and your loved ones able to sleep well at night and function well during the day, free from great worry about how you're going to meet next month's expenses?

- Are the likely rewards worth the risk that the borrowing entails?

- Are you and your loved ones financially able to save what you'd like to work toward your goals?

If you answer "no" to these questions, see the debt-reduction strategies in Chapter 7 for more information.

Analyze Your Savings

How much money have you actually saved in the past year? By that I mean the amount of new money you've added to your nest egg, stash, or whatever you like to call it.

Most people don't know or have only a vague idea of the rate at which they're saving money. The answer may sober, terrify, or pleasantly surprise you. In order to calculate your savings over the past year, you need to calculate your net worth as of today *and* as of one year ago.

The amount you actually saved over the past year is equal to the change in your net worth over the past year — in other words, your net worth today minus your net worth from one year ago. I know it may be a pain to find statements showing what your investments were worth a year ago, but bear with me: It's a useful exercise.

If you own your home, ignore this in the calculations. (However, you can consider the extra payments you make to pay off your mortgage principal faster as new savings.) And don't include personal property and consumer goods, such as your car, computer, clothing, and so on, with your assets. (See the earlier section "Determine Your Financial Net Worth" if you need more help with this task.)

When you have your net worth figures from both years, plug them into Step 1 of Table 2-4. If you're anticipating the exercise and are already subtracting your net worth of a year ago from what it is today to determine your rate of savings, your instincts are correct, but the exercise isn't quite that simple. You need to do a few more calculations in Step 2 of Table 2-4. Why? Well, counting the appreciation of the investments you've owned over the past year as savings wouldn't be fair. Suppose you bought 100 shares of a stock a year ago at $17 per share, and now the value is at $34 per share. Your investment increased in value by $1,700 during the past year. Although you'd be the envy of your friends at the next party if you casually mentioned your investments, the $1,700 of increased value is not really savings. Instead, it represents appreciation on your investments, so you must remove this appreciation from the calculations.

Step 1: Figuring your savings			
Today		**One Year Ago**	
Savings & investments	$_____	Savings & investments	$_____
– Loans & debts	$_____	– Loans & debts	$_____
= Net worth today	$_____	= Net worth 1 year ago	$_____
Step 2: Correcting for changes in value of investments you owned during the year			
Net worth today			$_____
– Net worth 1 year ago			$_____
– Appreciation of investments (over past year)			$_____
+ Depreciation of investments (over past year)			$_____
= Savings rate			$_____

Table 2-4: *Your Savings Rate over the Past Year*

If all this calculating gives you a headache, you get stuck, or you just hate crunching numbers, try the intuitive, seat-of-the-pants approach: Save a regular portion of your monthly income. You can save it in a separate savings or retirement account.

_____

_____

_____

How much do you save in a typical month? Get out the statements for accounts you contribute to or save money in monthly. It doesn't matter if you're saving money in a retirement account that you can't access — money is money.

Note: If you save, say, $200 per month for a few months, and then you spend it all on auto repairs, you're not really saving. If you contributed $5,000 to an individual retirement account (IRA), for example, but you depleted money that you had from long ago (in other words, money that wasn't saved during the past year), don't count the $5,000 IRA contribution as new savings.

Save at least 5 to 10 percent of your annual income for longer-term financial goals such as retirement. If you're not saving that much, be sure to read Chapter 9 to find out how to reduce your spending and increase your savings.

Assess Your Insurance Savvy

In this section, you have to deal with the prickly subject of protecting your assets and yourself with *insurance.* The following questions help you get started. Answer "yes" or "no" for each question.

_____ Do you understand the individual coverages, protection types, and amounts of each insurance policy you have?

_____ Does your current insurance protection make sense given your current financial situation (as opposed to your situation when you bought the policies)?

_____ If you wouldn't be able to make it financially without your income, do you have adequate long-term disability insurance coverage?

_____ If you have family members who are dependent on your continued income, do you have adequate life insurance coverage to replace your income if you die?

_____ Do you know when it makes sense to buy insurance through discount brokers, fee-for-service advisors, and companies that sell directly to the public (bypassing agents) and when it doesn't?

_____ Do you carry enough liability insurance on your home, car (including umbrella/excess liability), and business to protect all of your assets?

_____

_____

_____

_____ Have you recently (in the last year or two) shopped around for the best price on your insurance policies?

_____ Do you know whether your insurance companies have good track records when it comes to paying claims and keeping customers satisfied?

That wasn't so bad, was it? If you answered "no" more than once or twice, don't feel bad — nine out of ten people make significant mistakes when buying insurance. Find your insurance salvation in Chapter 11. If you answered "yes" to all the preceding questions, you can spare yourself from reading Chapter 11, but bear in mind that many people need as much help in this area as they do in other aspects of personal finance.

_____

_____

_____

3

Establishing Goals

In my work as a financial counselor, I always asked new clients what their short- and long-term personal and financial goals were. Most people reported that reflecting on this question was incredibly valuable because they hadn't considered it for a long time — if ever.

In this chapter, I help you dream about what you want to get out of life. Although my expertise is in personal finance, I wouldn't be doing my job if I didn't get you to consider your nonfinancial goals and how money fits into the rest of your life goals. So before I jump into how to establish and save toward common financial goals, I discuss how to think about making and saving money, as well as how to best fit your financial goals into the rest of your life.

A Definition of Wealth

Peruse any major financial magazine, newspaper, or website, and you'll quickly see our culture's obsession with financial wealth. The more money financial executives, movie stars, or professional athletes have, the more publicity and attention they seem to get.

I can tell you from my decades of working as a personal financial advisor and writer and interacting with folks from varied backgrounds that there's surprisingly little correlation between financial wealth and emotional wealth. That's why in your pursuit of financial wealth and security, you should always remember the emotional side. The following sections can help you gain some perspective.

What money can't buy

Recall the handful of best moments in your life. Odds are these times don't include the time you bought a car or found a designer sweater that you liked. The old saying is true: The most enjoyable and precious things of value in your life can't be bought.

_____

_____

_____

Money can't buy happiness. It's tempting to think that if you could only make 20 percent more or twice as much money, you'd be happier because you'd have more money to travel, eat out, and buy that new car you've been eyeing, right? Not so. A great deal of research suggests that little relationship exists between money and happiness.

Despite myriad technological gadgets and communication devices, cheap air travel, microwaves, personal computers, voice mail, smartphones, and all the other stuff that's supposed to make life easier and more enjoyable, Americans aren't any happier than they were five decades ago, according to research conducted by the National Opinion Research Center. These results occur even though incomes, after being adjusted for inflation, have more than doubled during that time.

The balancing act

Believe it or not, some people save too much. In my counseling practice, I saw plenty of people who fell into that category. If making and saving money are good things, then the more, the better, right? Well, take the extreme case of Anne Scheiber, who, on a modest income, started saving at a young age, allowing her money to compound in wealth-building investments such as stocks over many years. As a result, she was able to amass $20 million before she passed away at the age of 101.

Scheiber lived in a cramped studio apartment and never used her investments. She didn't even use the interest or dividends — she lived solely on her Social Security benefits and a small pension from her employer. Scheiber was extreme in her frugality and obsessed with her savings. As reported by James Glassman in *The Washington Post*, "She had few friends . . . she was an unhappy person, totally consumed by her securities accounts and her money." Most people, myself included, wouldn't choose to live and save the way that Scheiber did.

Even those who are saving for an ultimate goal can become consumed by their saving habits. Some people pursue higher-paying jobs and pinch pennies in order to retire early. But sometimes they make too many personal sacrifices today while chasing after some vision of their expected lives tomorrow. Others get consumed by work and then don't understand why their family and friends feel neglected — or don't even notice that they do.

Another problem with seeking to amass wealth is that tomorrow may not come. Even if all goes according to plan, will you know how to be happy when you're not working if

_____

_____

_____

you spend your entire life making money? More important, who will be around to share your leisure time? One of the costs of an intense career is time spent away from friends and family. You may realize your goal of retiring early, but you may be putting off too much living today in expectation of living tomorrow. As Charles D'Orleans said in 1465, "It's very well to be thrifty, but don't amass a hoard of regrets."

Of course, at the other extreme are spendthrifts who live only for today. A friend of mine once said, "I'm not into delayed gratification." "Shop 'til you drop" seems to be the motto of this personality type. "Why save when I might not be here tomorrow?" reasons this type of person.

The danger of this approach is that tomorrow may come after all, and most people don't want to spend all of their tomorrows working for a living. The earlier neglect of saving, however, may make it necessary for you to work when you're much older. And if for some reason you can't work and you have little money to live on, much less live enjoyably, the situation can be tragic. The only difference between a person without any savings or access to credit and some homeless people is a few months of unemployment.

Making and saving money are like eating food. If you don't eat enough, you may suffer. If you eat too much, the overage

_____

_____

_____

may go to waste or make you overweight. The right amount, perhaps with some extra to spare, affords you a healthy, balanced, peaceful existence. Money should be treated with respect and acknowledged for what it is — a means to an end and a precious resource that shouldn't be thoughtlessly squandered and wasted.

Find ways to make the most of the money that does pass through your hands, and never lose sight of all that is far more important than money.

Savings Goals

Most people I know have financial goals. The rest of this chapter discusses the most common financial goals and how to work toward them. See whether any of the following reflect your ambitions:

- **Owning your home:** Renting and dealing with landlords can be a financial and emotional drag, so most folks want to buy into the American dream and own some real estate — the most basic of which is your own home.

_____

_____

_____

- **Making major purchases:** Most folks need to plan ahead for major purchases such as a car, living room furniture, vacations, and so on.

- **Retiring:** No, retiring doesn't imply sitting in a rocking chair watching the world go by while hoping that some long-lost friend, your son or daughter's family, or the neighborhood dog comes by to visit. Retiring is a catch-all term for discontinuing full-time work or perhaps not even working for pay at all. (See Chapter 6 for more about retirement.)

- **Educating the kids:** All those diaper changes, late-night feedings, and trips to the zoo aren't enough to get Junior out of your house and into the real world as a productive, self-sufficient adult. You may want to help your children get a college education. Unfortunately, that can cost a truckload of dough.

- **Owning your own business:** Many employees want to take on the challenges and rewards that come with being the boss. The primary reason that most people continue just to dream is that they lack the money to leave their primary job. Although many businesses don't require gobs of start-up cash, almost all require

_____

_____

_____

that you withstand a substantial reduction in your income during the early years.

Because everyone is different, you can have goals (other than those in the preceding list) that are unique to your own situation. Accomplishing such goals almost always requires saving money. As one of my favorite Chinese proverbs says, "Do not wait until you are thirsty to dig a well," so don't wait to save money until you're ready to accomplish a personal or financial goal!

What's most important to you

Unless you earn really big bucks or have a large family inheritance to fall back on, your personal and financial desires will probably outstrip your resources. Thus, you must prioritize your goals.

One of the biggest mistakes people make is rushing into a financial decision without considering what's really important to them. Because many people get caught up in the responsibilities of their daily lives, they often don't have time for reflection.

People who accomplish their goals aren't necessarily smarter or higher-income earners than those who don't. People who identify their goals and then work toward them, which often requires changing some habits, are the ones who accomplish their goals.

Competing goals

Unless you enjoy paying higher taxes, why would you save money outside of retirement accounts, which shelter your money from taxation? The reason is that some financial goals are not easily achieved by saving in retirement accounts. Also, retirement accounts have caps on the amount you can contribute annually.

If you're accumulating money for a down payment on a home or to start or buy a business, for example, you'll probably need to save that money outside of a retirement account. Why? Because if you withdraw funds from retirement accounts before age 59½ and you're not retired, not only do you have to pay income taxes on the withdrawals, but you also generally have to pay *early withdrawal penalties* of 10 percent of the withdrawn amount in federal tax plus whatever your state charges.

_____

_____

_____

Because you're constrained by your financial resources, you need to prioritize your goals. Before funding your retirement accounts and racking up those tax breaks, read on to consider your other goals.

Emergency Reserves

Because you don't know what the future holds, preparing for the unexpected is financially wise. Even if you're the lucky sort who sometimes finds $5 bills on street corners, you can't control the chaotic world in which we live.

Conventional wisdom says you should have approximately six months of living expenses put away for an emergency. This particular amount may or may not be right for you because it depends, of course, on how expensive the emergency is. Why six months, anyway? And where should you put it?

 How much of an emergency stash you need depends on your situation. I recommend saving the following emergency amounts under differing circumstances:

_____

_____

_____

- **Three months' living expenses:** Choose this option if you have other accounts, such as a 401(k), or family members and close friends whom you can tap for a short-term loan. This minimalist approach makes sense when you're trying to maximize investments elsewhere (for example, in retirement accounts) or you have stable sources of income (employment or otherwise).

- **Six months' living expenses:** This amount is appropriate if you don't have other places to turn for a loan or you have some instability in your employment situation or source of income.

- **Up to one year's living expenses:** Set aside this much if your income fluctuates wildly from year to year or if your profession involves a high risk of job loss, finding another job could take you a long time, and you don't have other places to turn for a loan.

 In the event that your only current source of emergency funds is a high-interest credit card, first save at least three months' worth of living expenses in an accessible account before funding a retirement account or saving for other goals.

_____

_____

_____

Saving to Buy a Home or Business

When you're starting out financially, deciding whether to save money to buy a home or to put money into a retirement account presents a dilemma. In the long run, owning your own home is generally a wise financial move. On the other hand, saving sooner for retirement makes achieving your goals easier.

Presuming both goals are important to you, save toward both buying a home *and* for retirement. If you're eager to own a home, you can throw all of your savings toward achieving that goal and temporarily put your retirement savings on hold. Save for both purposes simultaneously if you're not in a rush.

You may be able to have the best of both worlds if you work for an employer that allows borrowing against retirement account balances. You can save money in the retirement account and then borrow against it for the down payment of a home. Be extra careful, though. Retirement account loans typically must be paid back within a set number of years (check with your employer) or immediately if you quit or lose your job. You're also allowed to make penalty-free withdrawals of up to $10,000 from individual retirement accounts toward a first-time home purchase.

When saving money for starting or buying a business, most people encounter the same dilemma they face when deciding to save to buy a house: If you fund your retirement accounts to the exclusion of earmarking money for your small-business dreams, your entrepreneurial aspirations may never become a reality. Generally, I advocate hedging your bets by saving money in your tax-sheltered retirement accounts as well as toward your business venture. An investment in your own small business can produce great rewards, so you may feel comfortable focusing your savings on your own business.

Educational Expenses

Wanting to provide for your children's future is perfectly natural, but doing so before you've saved adequately toward your own goals can be a major financial mistake. The college financial-aid system effectively penalizes you for saving money outside of retirement accounts and penalizes you even more if the money is invested in the child's name.

This concept may sound selfish, but you need to take care of *your* future first. Take advantage of saving through your tax-sheltered retirement accounts before you set aside money in custodial savings accounts for your kids. This practice isn't selfish: Do you really want to have to leech off your kids when you're old and frail because you didn't save any money for yourself?

Big Purchases

If you want to buy a car, a canoe, and a plane ticket to Thailand, do not, I repeat, do not buy such things with *consumer credit* (that is, carry debt month-to-month to finance the purchase on a credit card or auto loan). As I explain in Chapter 7, cars, boats, vacations, and the like are consumer items, not wealth-building investments, such as real estate or small businesses. A car begins to depreciate the moment you drive it off the sales lot. A plane ticket is worthless the moment you arrive back home.

_____

_____

_____

Don't deny yourself gratification; just learn how to delay it. Get into the habit of saving for your larger consumer purchases to avoid paying for them over time with high-interest consumer credit. When saving for a consumer purchase such as a car, a money-market account or short-term bond fund is a good place to store your short-term savings.

Paying for high-interest consumer debt can cripple your ability not only to save for long-term goals but also to make major purchases in the future. Interest on consumer debt is exorbitantly expensive — upwards of 20 percent on credit cards. When contemplating the purchase of a consumer item on credit, add up the total interest you'd end up paying on your debt and call it the price of instant gratification.

_____

_____

_____

4

Spending Habits

As a financial counselor, I've worked with people who have small incomes, people who have six-figure and even seven-figure incomes, and everyone in between. At every income level, people fall into one of the following categories:

- People who spend more than they earn (accumulating debt)
- People who spend all that they earn (saving nothing)
- People who save 2, 5, 10, or even 20 percent (or more!)

I've seen $40,000 earners who save 20 percent of their income ($8,000), $80,000 earners who save just 5 percent ($4,000), and people earning well into six figures annually who save nothing or accumulate debt.

Suppose you earn $50,000 per year and spend all of it. You may wonder, "How can I save money?" Good question!

Rather than work a second job, you may want to try living below your income — in other words, spending less than you earn. Consider that for every discontented person earning and spending $50,000 per year, someone else is out there making do on $45,000.

A great many people live on less than you make. If you spend as they do, you can save and invest the difference. In this chapter, I examine why people overspend and help you look at your own spending habits. When you know where your money goes, you can find ways to spend less and save more (see Chapter 9) so someday, you, too, can live richly and achieve your life's goals.

Overspending

If you're like most people, you must live within your means to accomplish your financial goals. Doing so requires spending less than you earn and then investing your savings intelligently. To put yourself in a position that allows you to start saving, take a close look at your spending habits.

Many folks earn just enough to make ends meet. And some can't even do that; they simply spend more than they make.

_____

_____

_____

The result of such spending habits is, of course, an accumulation of debt.

Most of the influences in society encourage you to spend. Think about it: More often than not, you're referred to as a *consumer* in the media and by politicians. You're not referred to as a person, a citizen, or a human being. This section looks at some of the adversaries you're up against as you attempt to control your spending.

Access to credit

As you probably already know, spending money is easy. Thanks to innovations like ATMs, credit cards, PayPal, and so on, your money is always available, 24/7.

Sometimes it may seem as though lenders are trying to give away money by making credit so easily available. But this free money is a dangerous illusion. Credit is most perilous when you make consumption purchases you can't afford in the first place. When it comes to consumer debt (credit cards, auto loans, and the like), lenders aren't giving away anything except the misfortune of getting in over your head, racking up high interest charges, and delaying your progress toward your financial and personal goals.

_____

_____

_____

Misusing credit cards

If you pay your bill in full every month, credit cards offer a convenient way to buy things with an interest-free, short-term loan. But if you carry debt over from month to month at high interest rates, credit cards encourage you to live beyond your means. Credit cards make it easy and tempting to spend money that you don't have.

You'll never pay off your credit card debt if you keep charging on your card and make only the minimum monthly payments. Interest continues to pile up on your outstanding debt. Paying only the minimum monthly payment can lead to carrying high-interest debt on your card for decades (not just months or years).

If you spend more than you should on your credit cards, only one solution exists: Get rid of your credit cards. Put scissors to the plastic. Go cold turkey. You can function without them. (See Chapter 7 for details on how to live without credit cards.)

Car loans

Walking onto a car lot and going home with a new car that you could never afford if you had to pay cash is easy. The dealer gets you thinking in terms of monthly payments that sound small when compared to what that vehicle is *really* going to cost you. Auto loans are easy for just about anyone to get.

Suppose you're tired of driving around in your old clunker. The car is battle-scarred and boring, and you don't like being seen in it. Plus, the car is likely to need more repairs in the months ahead and perhaps doesn't have all the safety features of newer models. So off you go to your local car dealer.

You start looking around at all the shiny, new cars, and then there it is: your new car. It's sleek and clean, and has air conditioning, an amazing stereo, a rearview camera, Bluetooth, and heated seats. Before you can read the fine print on the sticker page on the side window, the salesperson moseys on up next to you. He gets you talking about how nice the car is, the weather, or anything but the sticker price of that car.

"How can this guy afford to spend time with me without knowing if I can afford this thing?" you think. After a test drive and more talk about the car, the weather, and your love life comes your moment of truth. The salesperson, it seems, doesn't care about how much money you have. Whether you have lots of money or very little doesn't matter. The car is only $399 a month!

"That price isn't bad," you think. Heck, you were expecting to hear that the car would cost you at least 25 grand. Before you know it, the dealer runs a credit report on you and has you sign a few papers. Minutes later you're driving home with your new car.

The dealer wants you to think in terms of monthly payments because the cost *sounds* so cheap: $399 for a car. But, of course, that's $399 per month for many, many months. You're going to be paying forever — after all, you just bought a car that cost a huge chunk of your yearly take-home income.

But it gets worse. What does the total sticker price come to when interest charges are added in? (Even if interest charges are low, you may still be buying a car with a sticker price you can't afford.) And what about the cost of insurance, registration, and maintenance over the seven or so years that you'll probably own the car? Now you're probably up to more than a year's worth of your income. Ouch! (See Chapter 9 for information on how to spend what you can afford on a car.)

_____

_____

_____

Outside influences and agendas

You go out with some friends to dinner, a sporting event, or a show. Try to remember the last time one of you said, "Let's go someplace (or do something) less costly. I can't afford to spend this much." On the one hand, you don't want to be a stick in the mud. But on the other hand, some of your friends may have more money than you do — and the ones who don't may be running up debt fast.

Some people just have to see the latest hit movie, wear the latest designer clothes, or get the newest smartphone or tablet. They don't want to feel left out or behind the times.

When was the last time you heard someone say she decided to forgo a purchase because she was saving for retirement or a home purchase? It doesn't happen often, does it? Just dealing with the here-and-now and forgetting your long-term needs and goals is tempting. This mindset leads people to toil away for too many years in jobs they dislike.

Living for today has its virtues: Tomorrow *may* not come. But odds are good that it will. Will you still feel the same way about today's spending decisions tomorrow? Or will you feel guilty that you again failed to stick to your goals?

_____

_____

_____

Your spending habits should be driven by *your* desires and plans, not those of others. If you haven't set any goals yet, you may not know how much you should be saving. Chapter 3 helps you kick-start the planning and saving process.

Spending to feel good

Life is full of stress, obligations, and demands. "I work hard," you may say, "and darn it, I deserve to indulge!" Especially after your boss took the credit for your last great idea. So you buy something expensive or go to a fancy restaurant. Feel better? You won't when the bill arrives. And the more you spend, the less you save, and the longer you'll be stuck working for jerks like your boss!

Just as people can become addicted to alcohol, tobacco, television, and the Internet, some people also become addicted to the high they get from spending. Researchers can identify a number of psychological causes for a spending addiction, with some relating to how your parents handled money and spending.

If your spending and debt problems are chronic, or even if you'd simply like to be a better consumer and saver, see Chapter 7 for more information.

Analyze Your Spending

Brushing your teeth, eating a diverse diet including plenty of fruits and vegetables, and exercising regularly are good habits. Spending less than you earn and saving enough to meet your future financial objectives are the financial equivalents of these habits.

Despite relatively high incomes compared with the rest of the world, some Americans have a hard time saving a good percentage of their incomes. Why? Often it's because they spend too much — sometimes far more than necessary.

The first step to saving more of the income that you work so hard for is to figure out where that income typically gets spent. The spending analysis in the next section helps you determine where your cash is flowing. Do the spending analysis if any of the following apply to you:

• You aren't saving enough money to meet your financial goals. (If you're not sure whether this is the case, please see Chapter 3.)

- You feel as though your spending is out of control, or you don't know where all of your income goes.

- You're anticipating a significant life change (for example, marriage, having children, retiring, and so on).

If you're already a good saver, you may not need to complete the spending analysis. After you save enough to accomplish your goals, I don't see as much value in continually tracking your spending. You've already established the good habit — saving.

The immediate goal of a spending analysis is to figure out where you typically spend your money. The long-range goal is to establish a good habit: maintaining a regular, automatic savings routine.

Knowing where your money is going each month is useful, and making changes in your spending behavior and cutting out the fat so you can save more money and meet your financial goals is terrific. However, you may make yourself and those around you miserable if you're anal about documenting precisely where you spend every single dollar and cent. Saving what you need to achieve your goals is what matters most.

Low-tech methods to track your spending

Analyzing your spending is like being a detective. Your goal is to reconstruct the spending. You probably have some major clues at your fingertips or somewhere on the desk or computer where you handle your finances.

Unless you keep meticulous records that detail every dollar you spend, you won't have perfect information. Don't sweat it! A number of sources can enable you to detail where you've been spending your money. To get started, get out/access your

- Recent pay stubs
- Tax returns
- Online banking/bill payment record
- Log of checks paid and monthly debit card transactions
- Credit and charge card bills

Ideally, you want to assemble the information needed to track 12 months of spending. But if your spending patterns don't fluctuate greatly from month to month (or you won't complete the exercise if it means compiling a year's worth of data), you can reduce your data gathering to one six-month period or to every second or third month for the past year. If you take a major vacation or spend a large amount on gifts during certain months of the year, make sure you include these months in your analysis. Also account for insurance or other financial payments that you may choose not to pay monthly and instead pay quarterly, semiannually, or annually.

Purchases made with cash are the hardest to track because they don't leave a paper trail. Over the course of a week or perhaps even a month, you *could* keep a record of everything you buy with cash. Tracking cash can be an enlightening exercise, but it can also be tedious. (See the section "Digital means to track your spending" later in this chapter.) If you lack the time and patience, you can try *estimating.* Think about a typical week or month — how often do you buy things with cash? For example, if you eat lunch out four days a week, paying around $8 per meal, that's about $130 a month. You may also want to try adding up all the cash withdrawals from your checking account statement and then working backward to try to remember where you spent the cash.

Separate your expenditures into as many useful and detailed categories as possible. Table 4-1 gives you a suggested format; you can tailor it to fit your needs. Remember, if you lump too much of your spending into broad, meaningless categories like "Other," you'll end up right back where you started — wondering where all the money went. (*Note:* When completing the tax section in Table 4-1, report the total tax you paid for the year as tabulated on your annual income tax return — and take the total Social Security and Medicare taxes paid from your end-of-year pay stub — rather than the tax withheld or paid during the year.)

Category	Monthly Average ($)	Percent of Total Gross Income (%)
Taxes (income)		_____
FICA (Social Security & Medicare)	_____	
Federal	_____	
State and local	_____	
Housing and utilities		_____
Rent	_____	
Mortgage	_____	
Property taxes	_____	
Gas/electric/oil	_____	
Water/garbage	_____	
Phones	_____	
Cable TV & Internet	_____	
Gardener/housekeeper	_____	

Table 4-1: *Detailing Your Spending*

(continued)

Category	Monthly Average ($)	Percent of Total Gross Income (%)
Furniture/appliances	_____	
Maintenance/repairs	_____	
Food		_____
Supermarket	_____	
Restaurants and takeout	_____	
Transportation		_____
Gasoline	_____	
Maintenance/repairs	_____	
State registration fees	_____	
Tolls and parking	_____	
Bus or subway fares	_____	
Style		_____
Clothing	_____	
Shoes	_____	
Jewelry (watches, earrings)	_____	
Dry cleaning	_____	
Debt repayments (excluding mortgage)		_____
Credit/charge cards	_____	
Auto loans	_____	
Student loans	_____	
Other	_____	

Table 4-1: *(continued)*

Category	Monthly Average ($)	Percent of Total Gross Income (%)
Fun stuff		_____
Entertainment (movies, concerts)	_____	
Vacation and travel	_____	
Gifts	_____	
Hobbies	_____	
Subscriptions/memberships	_____	
Pets	_____	
Other	_____	
Personal care		_____
Haircuts	_____	
Health club or gym	_____	
Makeup	_____	
Other	_____	
Personal business		_____
Accountant/attorney/financial advisor	_____	
Other	_____	
Health care		_____
Physicians and hospitals	_____	
Drugs	_____	
Dental and vision	_____	
Therapy	_____	

(continued)

Category	Monthly Average ($)	Percent of Total Gross Income (%)
Insurance		_____
Homeowners/renters	_____	
Auto	_____	
Health	_____	
Life	_____	
Disability	_____	
Long-term care	_____	
Umbrella liability	_____	
Educational expenses		_____
Tuition	_____	
Books	_____	
Supplies	_____	
Housing costs (room & board)	_____	
Children		_____
Day care	_____	
Toys	_____	
Activities	_____	
Child support	_____	
Charitable donations	_____	_____
Other		_____
_____	_____	
_____	_____	
_____	_____	

Table 4-1: *(continued)*

Digital means to track your spending

Software programs and websites can assist you with paying bills and tracking your spending. The main advantage of using software or websites is that you can continually track your spending as long as you keep entering the information. Software packages and websites can even help speed up the check-writing process.

But you don't need a computer and fancy software to pay your bills and figure out where you're spending money. Many people stop entering data after a few months. If tracking your spending is what you're after, you need to enter information from the bills you pay by check and the expenses you pay by credit card and cash. Such software often ends up in the consumer graveyard.

Plenty of websites and apps are devoted to supposedly helping you to reduce your spending. But consumer beware. These digital means have inherent problems, which I cover in detail in Chapter 12.

Paper, pencil, and a calculator can work just fine for tracking your spending. For those who want to use technology to track bill payments and expenses, I recommend the best software packages in Chapter 12.

5

Credit Scores
and Reports

You likely have a personal credit report and a credit score. Lenders examine your credit report and score before granting you a loan or credit line. This chapter highlights what you need to know about your credit score and reports, including how to obtain them and how to improve them.

Credit Data

A *credit report* contains information such as

- **Personal identifying information:** Includes your name, address, Social Security number, and so on

- **Record of credit accounts:** Details when each account was opened, the latest balance, your payment history, and so on

- **Bankruptcy filings:** Indicates whether you've filed bankruptcy in recent years

- **Inquiries:** Lists who has pulled your credit report because you applied for credit

Your *credit score*, which is not the same as your credit report, is a three-digit score based on the report. Lenders use your credit score as a predictor of your likelihood of defaulting on repaying your borrowings. As such, your credit score has a major impact on whether a lender is willing to extend you a particular loan and at what interest rate.

FICO, developed by Fair Isaac and Company, is the leading credit score in the industry. FICO scores range from a low of 300 to a high of 850. Most scores fall in the 600s and 700s. As with college entrance examinations, higher scores are better.

The higher your credit score, the lower your predicted likelihood of defaulting on a loan (see Figure 5-1). The "rate of credit delinquency" refers to the percentage of consumers who will become 90 days late or later in repaying a creditor within the next two years. As you can see in the chart, consumers with low credit scores have dramatically higher rates of falling behind on their loans. Thus, people with low credit scores are considered much riskier borrowers, and fewer lenders are willing to offer them a given loan; those who do offer loans charge relatively high interest rates.

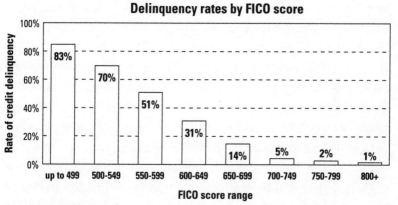

Delinquency rates by FICO score

Source: Fair Isaac Corporation

Figure 5-1: *Lenders use credit scores to estimate how likely people are to default on a loan.*

The median FICO score is around 720. You generally qualify for the best lending rates if your credit score is in the mid-700s or higher.

Obtaining Your Credit Reports and Score

Given the importance of your personal credit report, you may be pleased to know that federal law entitles you to receive a free copy of your credit report annually from each of the three credit bureaus (Equifax, Experian, and TransUnion).

If you visit www.annualcreditreport.com, you can view and print copies of your credit report from each of the three credit agencies online (alternatively, call 877-322-8228 to have your reports mailed to you). After entering some personal data at the website, check the box indicating that you want to obtain all three credit reports because each report may have slightly different information. You'll then be directed to one of the three bureaus, and after you finish verifying that you are who you claim to be at that site, you can easily navigate back to www.annualcreditreport.com so you can continue to the next agency's site.

When you receive your reports, the best first step is to examine them for possible mistakes (see the upcoming section "Credit Report Errors" to find out how to fix problems in your reports).

_____

_____

_____

In the past, I found minor errors on two of the three reports. It took me several minutes to correct one of the errors (by submitting a request to that credit reporting agency's website), and it took about half an hour to get the other mistake fixed.

You may be surprised to find that your credit reports do *not* include your credit score. The reason for this is quite simple: The 2003 law mandating that the three credit agencies provide a free credit report annually to each US citizen who requests a copy did not mandate that they provide the credit score. Thus, if you want to obtain your credit score, it's going to cost you.

You can request your credit score from Fair Isaac, but you'll get charged $19.95 for every request (that can set you back nearly $60 to see your FICO score for all three credit bureaus). Save your money. Many banks and credit cards offer free access to credit scores, and some even provide your updated score on a monthly basis. Call your bank or credit card to see if they offer this service. If they don't, you can order your credit score from the individual credit bureaus when you obtain your credit report(s) via www. annualcreditreport.com — Equifax, for example, charges just $7.95 to obtain your current credit score.

Improving Your Credit Reports and Score

If you don't like what you see when you obtain your credit reports and score, take time to improve your credit standing and score. Working to boost your credit rating is especially worthwhile if you know that your credit report contains detrimental information.

Here are the most important actions you can take to boost your attractiveness to lenders:

- **Get all three of your credit reports, and be sure each is accurate.** Correct errors (see the next section) and be especially sure to get accounts removed if they aren't yours and they show late payments or are in collection.

- **Ask to have any late or missed payments that are more than seven years old removed.** The same goes for a bankruptcy that occurred more than ten years ago.

- **Pay all your bills on time.** To ensure on-time payments, sign up for automatic bill payment, a service that most companies (like phone and utility providers) offer.

- **Be loyal if it doesn't cost you.** The older your open loan accounts are, the better your credit rating will be. Closing old accounts and opening a bunch of new ones generally lowers your credit score. But don't be loyal if it costs you! For example, if you can refinance your mortgage and save some money, by all means do so. The same logic applies if you're carrying credit card debt at a high interest rate and want to transfer that balance to a lower-rate card. If your current credit card provider refuses to match a lower rate you find elsewhere, move your balance and save yourself some money (see Chapter 7 for details).

- **Limit your debt and debt accounts.** The more loans, especially consumer loans, that you hold and the higher the balances, the lower your credit score will be.

- **Work to pay down consumer revolving debt (such as credit card debt).** Turn to Chapters 7 and 9 for suggestions.

Correcting Credit Report Errors

If you obtain your credit report and find a blemish on it that you don't recognize as being your mistake or fault, do *not* assume that the information is correct. Credit reporting bureaus and the creditors who report credit information to these bureaus often make errors.

You hope and expect that if a credit bureau has negative and incorrect information in your credit report and you bring the mistake to their attention, they will graciously and expeditiously fix the error. Think again.

You're going to have to fill out a form on a website, make some phone calls, or write a letter or two to fix the problems on your credit report. Here's how to correct most errors that aren't your fault:

- **If the credit problem is someone else's:** A surprising number of personal credit report glitches are the result of someone else's negative information getting on your credit report. If the bad information on your report doesn't look familiar to you, contact the credit bureau (by phone or online) and explain that you need more information because you don't recognize the creditor.

- **If the creditor made a mistake:** Creditors make mistakes, too. You need to write or call the creditor to get it to correct the erroneous information that it sent to the credit bureau. Phoning first usually works best. (The credit bureau should be able to tell you how to reach the creditor if you don't know how.) If necessary, follow up with a letter.

Whether you speak with a credit bureau or an actual lender, make note of your conversations. If representatives say they can fix the problem, get their names, email addresses, and phone extensions, and follow up with them if they don't deliver as promised. If you're ensnared in bureaucratic red tape, escalate the situation by speaking with a department manager. By law, bureaus are required to respond to a request to fix a credit error within 30 days. Hold the bureau accountable!

Tell your side of the story

With a minor credit infraction, some lenders may simply ask for an explanation. Years ago, I had a credit report blemish that was the result of being away for several weeks and missing the payment due date for a couple of small bills. When my proposed mortgage lender saw my late payments, the lender asked for a simple written explanation.

You and a creditor may not see eye to eye on a problem, and the creditor may refuse to budge. If that's the case, credit bureaus are required by law to allow you to add a 100-word explanation to your credit file.

Sidestep "credit repair" firms

Online and in newspapers and magazines, you may see ads for credit repair companies that claim to fix your credit report problems. In the worst cases I've seen, these firms charge outrageous amounts of money and don't come close to fulfilling their marketing hype.

If you have legitimate glitches on your credit report, credit repair firms can't make the glitches disappear. Hope springs eternal, however — some people would like to believe that their credit problems can be fixed.

If your problems are fixable, you can fix them yourself; you don't need to pay a credit repair company big bucks to do it.

_____

_____

_____

6

Retirement

Many people aspire to retire sooner rather than later. But this idea has some problems. If you want to retire by your mid-60s (when Social Security kicks in), you need to save enough money to support yourself for 20 to 30 years, maybe longer. Two to three decades is a long time to live off your savings. You're going to need a good-sized chunk of money — more than most people realize.

The earlier you hope to retire, the more money you need to set aside and the sooner you have to start saving — unless you plan to work part time in retirement to earn more income!

Many of the people I speak to say they do want to retire, and most say "the sooner, the better." Yet more than half of Americans between the ages of 18 and 34, and a quarter of those ages 35 to 54, haven't begun to save for retirement. When I asked one of my middle-aged counseling clients, who had saved little for retirement, when he would like to retire, he deadpanned, "Sometime before I die."

This chapter helps you determine where you stand financially regarding retirement. If you're like most working people, you need to increase your savings rate for retirement.

How Much You Need for Retirement

If you hope to someday reduce the time you spend working or cease working altogether, you'll need sufficient savings to support yourself. Many people — particularly young people and those who don't work well with numbers — underestimate the amount of money needed to retire. To figure out how much you should save per month to achieve your retirement goals, you need to do some calculating.

Most people need about 70 to 80 percent of their pre-retirement income throughout retirement to maintain their standard of living. For example, if your household earns $50,000 per year before retirement, you're likely to need $35,000 to $40,000 (70 to 80 percent of $50,000) per year during retirement to live the way you're accustomed to living. The

70 to 80 percent is an average. Some people may need more simply because they have more time on their hands to spend their money. Others adjust their standard of living and live on less.

So how do you figure out what you're going to need? The following three profiles provide a rough estimate of the percentage of your pre-retirement income you're going to need during retirement. Pick the one that most accurately describes your situation. If you fall between two descriptions, pick a percentage in between those two.

To maintain your standard of living in retirement, you may need about

- **65 percent of your pre-retirement income if you**
  - Save a large amount (15 percent or more) of your annual earnings
  - Are a high-income earner
  - Will own your home free of debt by the time you retire
  - Do not anticipate leading a lifestyle in retirement that reflects your current high income

_____

_____

_____

If you're an especially high-income earner who lives well beneath your means, you may be able to do just fine with even less than 65 percent. Pick an annual dollar amount or percentage of your current income that will allow the kind of retirement lifestyle you desire.

- **75 percent of your pre-retirement income if you**
  - Save a reasonable amount (5 to 14 percent) of your annual earnings
  - Will still have some mortgage debt or a modest rent to pay by the time you retire
  - Anticipate having a standard of living in retirement that's comparable to what you have today

- **85 percent of your pre-retirement income if you**
  - Save little or none of your annual earnings (less than 5 percent)
  - Will have a relatively significant mortgage payment or sizeable rent to pay in retirement
  - Anticipate wanting or needing to maintain your current lifestyle throughout retirement

_____

_____

_____

Tax Advantages

Retirement accounts offer you a tax advantage. These accounts — known by such enlightening acronyms and names as 401(k), 403(b), SEP-IRAs, and so on — offer tax breaks to people of all economic means. Consider the following advantages to investing in retirement accounts:

- **Contributions are usually tax deductible.** By putting money in a retirement account, not only do you plan wisely for your future, but you also get an immediate financial reward: lower taxes, which means more money available for saving and investing. Retirement account contributions generally aren't taxed at either the federal or state income tax level until withdrawal (but they're still subject to Social Security and Medicare taxes when earned). If you're paying 35 percent between federal and state taxes (see Chapter 10 to determine your tax bracket), a $5,000 contribution to a retirement account lowers your taxes by $1,750.

- **In some company retirement accounts, companies match a portion of your contributions.** Thus, in addition to tax breaks, you get free extra money courtesy of your employer.

- **Returns on your investment compound over time without taxation.** After you put money into a retirement account, any interest, dividends, and appreciation add to your account without being taxed. Of course, these accounts don't allow for complete tax avoidance. Yet they do have an upside: You get to defer taxes on all the accumulating gains and profits until you withdraw the money down the road. Thus, more money is working for you over a longer period of time.

Retirement Building Blocks

When preparing financially for retirement, you need a basic foundation so your necessary retirement reserves can grow. If you've been working steadily, you may already have a good foundation, even if you haven't been actively saving toward retirement. In the pages ahead, I walk you through the probable components of your future retirement income and show you how to figure how much you should be saving to reach particular retirement goals.

_____

_____

_____

Social Security

According to polls, about half of American adults under the age of 35, and more than a third of those between the ages of 35 and 49, think that Social Security benefits will not be available by the time they retire.

Contrary to widespread skepticism, Social Security should be available when you retire, no matter how old you are today. In fact, Social Security is one of the sacred cow political programs.

If you think you can never retire because you don't have any money saved, I'm happy to inform you that you're probably wrong. You likely have some Social Security. But Social Security generally isn't enough to live on comfortably.

Social Security is intended to provide you with a subsistence level of retirement income for the basic necessities: food, shelter, and clothing. Social Security is not intended to be your sole source of income. Some of the elderly are quite dependent on Social Security: It's the only source of income for 21 percent of the elderly, and about two out of three Social Security recipients derive at least half of their total retirement income from their Social Security retirement check. Few working people can maintain their current lifestyles into retirement without supplementing Social Security with personal savings and company retirement plans.

_____

_____

_____

How much work makes me eligible?

To be eligible to collect Social Security benefits, you need to have worked a minimum number of 40 calendar quarters to qualify for Social Security retirement benefits.

If, for some reason, you work only the first half of a year or only during the summer months, don't despair. You don't need to work part of every quarter to get a quarter's credit. You get credits based on the income you earn during the year. As of this writing, you get the full four quarters credited to your account if you earn $4,880 or more ($1,220 per credit) in a year. To get 40 quarters of coverage, you basically need to work (at least portions of) ten years.

To get credits, your income must be reported, and you must pay taxes on it (including Social Security tax). In other words, you and those you employ encounter problems when you neglect to declare income or you pay people under the table; you may be cheating yourself, or others, out of valuable benefits.

How much will I get from Social Security?

The average monthly benefit Social Security pays out to retirees is about $1,328. The higher your employment earnings have been on average, the more you can expect to receive. If you're married and one of you doesn't work for pay, the nonworking spouse collects 50 percent of what the working spouse collects. Working spouses are eligible for either individual benefits or half of their spouse's benefits — whichever amount is greater.

To get a more precise handle on your Social Security benefits, visit the Social Security Administration (SSA) website at www.ssa.gov or call the SSA at 800-772-1213 and ask for Form 7004, which allows you to receive a record of your reported earnings and an estimate of your Social Security benefits. Check your earnings record because occasional errors do arise and — surprise — they usually aren't in your favor.

Plan your personal savings strategy

Money you're saving toward retirement can include money under the mattress as well as money in a retirement account such as an individual retirement account (IRA), 401(k), or similar plan. You may also earmark investments in nonretirement accounts for your retirement.

Equity (the difference between the market value less any mortgage balances owed) in rental or investment real estate can

_____

_____

_____

be counted toward your retirement as well. Deciding whether to include the equity in your primary residence (your home) is trickier. If you don't want to count on using this money in retirement, don't include it when you tally your stash.

You may want to count a portion of your home equity in your total assets for retirement. Some people sell their homes when they retire and move to a lower-cost area, move closer to family, or downsize to a more manageable-size home.

Make the most of employer-sponsored plans

Many employers set up retirement plans for their employees and provide a limited number of investment options. All you have to do is contribute and choose how to divide your money among the menu of investment choices.

401(k) plans

For-profit companies offer *401(k) plans*. A 401(k) generally allows you to save up to $18,000 per year (for 2017), usually through payroll deductions. If you're age 50 or older, you can stash away even more — $24,000 (for 2017). Your employer's plan may have lower limits, though. Your contributions to a 401(k) are excluded from your reported income and thus are generally free from federal and state income taxes (although they are subject to Social Security and Medicare taxes). Future year limits will increase in $500 increments to keep pace with inflation.

Some employers don't allow you to contribute to a 401(k) plan until you work for them for a full year. Others allow you to start contributing right away. Some employers also match a portion of your contributions. They may, for example, match half of your first 6 percent of contributions; so in addition to saving a lot of taxes, you get a bonus from the company.

If you're a high-income earner and you contribute such a significant percentage of each paycheck that you hit the plan maximum before the end of the year, you may lose out on some matching money. You may be better off spreading your contributions over the full calendar year. Check with your company's benefits department for your plan's specifics.

403(b) plans

Nonprofit organizations offer *403(b) plans* to their employees. As with 401(k)s, your contributions to these plans are excluded from federal and state income taxes. The 403(b) plans are often called *tax-sheltered annuities,* the name for insurance company investments that satisfy the requirements for 403(b) plans.

_____

_____

_____

Nonprofit employees are allowed to annually contribute up to $18,000 of their salary ($24,000 if age 50 or older) for tax year 2017. (Future year limits will increase with the cost of living in $500 increments.) Employees who have 15 or more years of service may be allowed to contribute beyond the standard limits. Ask your employee benefits department or the investment provider for the 403(b) plan about eligibility requirements and the details of your personal contribution limit.

If you work for a nonprofit or public-sector organization that doesn't offer this benefit, lobby for it. Nonprofit organizations have no excuse not to offer a 403(b) plan to their employees. Unlike a 401(k), this type of plan requires virtually no out-of-pocket expenses from the employer. The only requirement is that the organization must deduct the appropriate contribution from employees' paychecks and send the money to the investment company handling the 403(b) plan.

With some 403(b) plans, you may borrow against your fund balance without penalty. If this capability is important to you, check with your employer to see whether the company plan allows loans. Although many insurance annuities advertise borrowing as an advantage, it can also be a drawback because it may encourage you to raid your retirement money.

Estimate Your Retirement Savings

Now that you've toured the components of your future retirement income, take a shot at tallying where you stand in terms of retirement preparations. Don't be afraid to do this exercise — it's not difficult, and you may find that you're not in such bad shape. I even explain how to catch up if you find that you're behind in saving for retirement.

Note: The following worksheet (Table 6-1) and the Growth Multiplier (Table 6-2) assume that you're going to retire at age 66 and that your investments will produce an annual rate of return that is 4 percent higher than the rate of inflation. (For example, if inflation averages 3 percent, this table assumes that you will earn 7 percent per year on your investments.)

Retirement Income or Needs	Amount
1. Annual retirement income needed in today's dollars (see earlier in this chapter)	$ _____ / year
2. Annual Social Security	– $ _____ / year
3. Annual retirement income needed from personal savings (subtract line 2 from line 1)	= $ _____ / year
4. Savings needed to retire at age 66 (multiply line 3 by 15)	$ _____
5. Value of current retirement savings (including employer-sponsored plan)	$ _____
6. Value of current retirement savings at retirement (multiply line 5 by Growth Multiplier in Table 6-2)	$ _____
7. Amount you still need to save (line 4 minus line 6)	$ _____
8. Amount you need to save per month (multiply line 7 by Savings Factor in Table 6-2)	$ _____ / month

Table 6-1: *Retirement Planning Worksheet*

Your Current Age	Growth Multiplier	Savings Factor
26	4.8	0.001
28	4.4	0.001
30	4.1	0.001
32	3.8	0.001
34	3.5	0.001
36	3.2	0.001
38	3.0	0.002

Table 6-2: *Growth Multiplier*

(continued)

Your Current Age	Growth Multiplier	Savings Factor
40	2.8	0.002
42	2.6	0.002
44	2.4	0.002
46	2.2	0.003
48	2.0	0.003
50	1.9	0.004
52	1.7	0.005
54	1.6	0.006
56	1.5	0.007
58	1.4	0.009
60	1.3	0.013
62	1.2	0.020
64	1.1	0.041

Table 6-2: *(continued)*

Make Up for Lost Time

If the amount you need to save per month to reach your retirement goals seems daunting, all is not lost. Here are my top recommendations for making up for lost time:

- **Question your spending.** You have two ways to boost your savings: Earn more money or cut your spending (or do both). Most people don't spend their money nearly as thoughtfully as they earn it. See Chapter 9 for suggestions and strategies for reducing your spending.

- **Be more realistic about your retirement age.** If you extend the age at which you plan to retire, you get a double benefit: You earn and save money for more years, and you spend your nest egg over fewer years. Of course, if your job is making you crazy, this option may not be too appealing. Try to find work that makes you happy, and consider working, at least part time, during your "early" retirement years.

- **Use your home equity.** The prospect of tapping the cash in your home can be troubling. After getting together the down payment, you probably worked for many years to pay off your mortgage. But what's the use of owning a house free of mortgage debt when you lack sufficient retirement reserves? The money that's tied up in the house can be used to help increase your standard of living in retirement.

  You have a number of ways to tap your home's equity. You can sell your home and either move to a lower-cost property or rent an apartment. Current tax laws allow you to realize up to $250,000 in tax-free profit from the sale of your house ($500,000 if you're married). Another option is a reverse mortgage, in which you get a monthly income check as you build a loan balance against the value of your home. The loan is paid when your home is finally sold.

- **Grow your investments.** The faster the rate at which your money grows and compounds, the less you need to save each year to reach your goals. (Make sure, however, that you're not reckless; don't take huge risks in the hopes of big returns.) Earning just a few extra percentage points per year on your investments can dramatically slash the amount you need to save. The younger you are, the more powerful the effect of compounding interest. For example, if you're in your mid-30s and your investments appreciate 6 percent per year (rather than 4 percent) faster than the rate of inflation, the amount you need to save each month to reach your retirement goals drops by about 40 percent.

- **Turn a hobby into supplemental retirement income.** Even if you earn a living in the same career over many decades, you have skills that are portable and can be put to profitable use. Pick something you enjoy and are good at, develop a business plan, and get smart about how to market your services and wares. Remember, as people get busier, more specialized services are created to support their hectic lives. A demand for quality, homemade goods of all varieties also exists. Be creative!

- **Invest to gain tax-free and other free money.** By investing in a tax-wise fashion, you can boost the effective rate of return on your investments without taking on additional risk.

  In addition to the tax benefits you gain from funding most types of retirement accounts, some employers offer free matching money. Also, the government now offers tax credits (see Chapter 10) for low- and moderate-income earners who use retirement accounts.

  As for money outside of tax-sheltered retirement accounts, if you're in a relatively high tax bracket, you may earn more by investing in tax-free investments and other vehicles that minimize highly taxed distributions.

- **Think about inheritances.** Although you should never count on an inheritance to support your retirement, you may inherit money someday. If you want to see what impact an inheritance has on your retirement calculations, add a conservative estimate of the amount you expect to inherit to your current total savings in Table 6-1.

_____

_____

_____

7

Reducing Your Spending

Telling people how and where to spend their money is a risky undertaking because most people like to spend money and hate to be told what to do. So in this chapter I detail numerous strategies that I have seen work for other people. The final decision for what to cut rests solely on you. Only you can decide what's important to you and what's dispensable (should you cut out your weekly poker games or cut back on your shoe collection?).

With these recommendations, I assume that you value your time. Therefore, I don't tell you to scrimp and save by doing things like cutting open a tube of toothpaste so you can use every last bit of it. And I don't tell you to have your spouse do your ironing to reduce your dry cleaning bills — no point in having extra money in the bank if your significant other walks out on you!

The fact that you're busy may be part of the reason you spend money as you do. Therefore, the recommendations in this chapter focus on methods that produce significant savings but don't involve a lot of time.

Keys to Successful Spending

For most people, spending money is a whole lot easier and more fun than earning it. Far be it from me to tell you to stop having fun and turn into a penny-pinching, stay-at-home miser. Of course you can spend money. But there's a world of difference between spending money carelessly and spending money *wisely*.

If you spend too much and spend unwisely, you put pressure on your income and your future need to continue working. Savings dwindle, debts may accumulate, and you can't achieve your financial (and perhaps personal) goals.

If you dive into details too quickly, you may miss the big picture. So before I jump into the specific areas where you can trim your budget, I give you my four keys to successful spending. These four principles run through my recommendations in this chapter:

- Living within your means
- Finding the best values
- Cutting excess spending
- Rejecting consumer credit

Live within your means

Spending too much is a *relative* problem. Two people can each spend $40,000 per year yet still have drastically different financial circumstances. How? Suppose one of them earns $50,000 annually, while the other makes $35,000. The $50,000 income earner saves $10,000 each year. The $35,000 wage earner, on the other hand, accumulates $5,000 of new debt (or spends that amount from prior savings). So spend within your means. If you do nothing else in this chapter, please be sure to do this!

 Don't let the spending habits of others dictate yours. Certain people bring out the big spender in you. Do something else with them besides shopping and spending. If you can't find any other activity to share

_____

_____

_____

with them, try shopping with limited cash and no credit cards. That way you can't overspend on impulse.

Look for the best values

You can find high quality and low cost in the same product. Conversely, paying a high price is no guarantee that you're getting high quality. Cars are a good example. Whether you're buying a subcompact, a sports car, or a luxury four-door sedan, some cars are more fuel-efficient and cheaper to maintain than rivals that carry the same sticker price.

When you evaluate the cost of a product or service, think in terms of total long-term costs. Suppose you're comparing the purchase of two used cars: the Solid Sedan, which costs $11,995, and the Clunker Convertible, which is priced at $9,995. On the surface, the convertible appears to be cheaper. However, the price you pay for a car is but a small portion of what that car ultimately costs you. If the convertible is costly to operate, maintain, and insure over the years, it could end up costing you much more than the sedan would. Sometimes, paying a reasonable amount more upfront for a higher-quality product or service ends up saving you money in the long run.

Cut excess spending

If you want to reduce your overall spending by, say, 10 percent, you can cut all of your current expenditures by 10 percent. Or, you can reach your 10 percent goal by cutting some categories a lot and others not at all. You need to set priorities and make choices about where you want and don't want to spend your money.

What you spend your money on is sometimes a matter of habit rather than a matter of what you really want or value. For example, some people shop at whatever stores are close to them. But eliminating fat doesn't necessarily mean cutting back on your purchases: You can save money by buying in bulk. Some stores specialize in selling larger packages or quantities of a product at a lower price because they save money on the packaging and handling. If you're single, shop with a friend and split the bulk purchases.

Reject consumer credit

Buying items that depreciate — such as cars, clothing, and vacations — on credit is hazardous to your long-term financial health. Buy only what you can afford today. If you'll be forced to carry a debt for months or years on end, you can't really afford what you're buying on credit today.

Consumer credit is expensive, and it reinforces a bad financial habit: spending more than you can afford.

Budget to Boost Your Savings

When most people hear the word *budgeting,* they think unpleasant thoughts, and rightfully so. But budgeting can help you move from knowing how much you spend on various things to successfully reducing your spending.

The first step in the process of *budgeting,* or planning your future spending, is to analyze where your current spending is going (refer to Chapter 4). After you do that, calculate how much more you'd like to save each month. Then comes the hard part: deciding where to make cuts in your spending.

Suppose you're currently not saving any of your monthly income and you want to save 10 percent for retirement. If you can save and invest through a tax-sheltered retirement account — for example, a 401(k) or 403(b) — you don't need to cut your spending by 10 percent to reach a savings goal of 10 percent (of your gross income). When you contribute money to a tax-deductible retirement account, you reduce your federal and state taxes. If you're a moderate-income earner paying, say, 30 percent in federal and state taxes on your marginal income, you actually need to reduce your spending by only 7 percent to save 10 percent. The other 3 percent of the savings comes from the lowering of your taxes. (The higher your tax bracket, the less you need to cut your spending to reach a particular savings goal.)

So to boost your savings rate to 10 percent, go through your current spending category by category until you come up with enough proposed cuts to reduce your spending by 8 percent. Make your cuts in the areas that will be the least painful and where you're getting the least value from your current level of spending. (If you don't have access to a tax-deductible retirement account, budgeting still involves the same process of assessment and making cuts in various spending categories, but your cuts need to add up to the entire amount you want to save, in this example, 10 percent rather than 8 percent.)

Another method of budgeting involves starting from scratch rather than examining your current expenses and making cuts from that starting point. Ask yourself how much you'd like to spend on different categories. The advantage of this approach is that it doesn't allow your current spending levels to constrain your thinking. You'll likely be amazed at the discrepancies between what you think you should be spending and what you actually are spending in certain categories.

Reduce Your Spending

As you read through the following strategies for reducing your spending, please keep in mind that some of these strategies will make sense for you and some of them won't. Start your spending reduction plan with the strategies that come easily. Work your way through them. Keep a list of the options that are more challenging for you — ones that may require more of a sacrifice but may be workable if necessary to achieve your spending and savings goals.

No matter which of the ideas in this chapter you choose, rest assured that keeping your budget lean and mean pays enormous dividends. After you implement a spending reduction strategy, you'll reap the benefits for years to come. Take a look at Figure 7-1: For every $1,000 you shave from your annual spending (that's just $83 per month), check out how much more money you'll have down the road. (This chart assumes that you invest your newfound savings in a tax-deferred retirement account, you average 8-percent-per-year returns on your investments, and you're in a combined federal and state tax bracket of 35 percent — see Chapter 10 for information on tax brackets.)

Food costs

Not eating is one way to reduce food expenditures; however, this method tends to make you weak and dizzy, so it's probably not a viable long-term strategy. The following culinary cutbacks can help you save money.

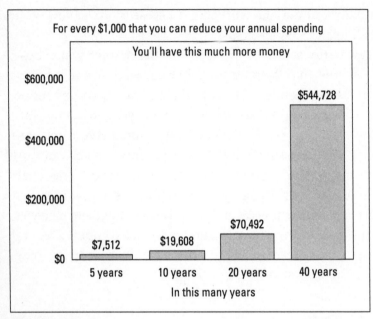

For every $1,000 that you can reduce your annual spending

You'll have this much more money

Figure 7-1: *Reducing your spending can yield large investment sums.*

Eating out frugally

Eating meals out and getting takeout can be timesavers, but they rack up big bills if done too often and too lavishly. Eating out is a luxury — think of it as hiring someone to shop, cook, and clean up for you. Of course, some people hate to cook or don't have the time, space, or energy to do much in the kitchen.

_____

_____

_____

If this sounds like you, choose restaurants carefully and order from the menu selectively. When eating out, avoid ordering beverages, especially alcohol, because of their pricey markup. Also consider ordering vegetarian dishes, which are usually less expensive than meat entrees.

 If you aren't skilled in the kitchen, consider learning how to cook. Folks who eat out a lot do so in part because they don't really know how to cook. Take a cooking class and read some good books on the topic.

Eating healthy at home without spending a fortune

As evidenced by the preponderance of diet and weight-loss books on bestseller lists — and the growth of natural and organic grocery stores like Whole Foods and Trader Joe's — Americans are trying to eat healthier. Concerned about all the pesticides, antibiotics, and hormones that end up in the food supply, more and more consumers are filling their kitchens with organic food.

Problem is, financially speaking, better quality food, especially organic foods, can cost more, sometimes much more — but not always. A number of studies demonstrate that highly processed foods, which are less nutritious and worse for your health, can be as costly as or even more expensive than fresh, so-called whole foods. The key to not overspending on fresher, healthier, and organic foods is to be flexible when you're at the grocery store. Buy more of what is seasonal and therefore currently less expensive, stock up on sale items that aren't perishable, and buy more at stores like Trader Joe's that have competitive pricing. Many larger grocery chains carry some organic foods; just be sure to comparison price.

One area where many folks are wasting money is in buying bottled water. Although tap water often does leave something to be desired, bottled water is typically not as pure as some folks think. You can save hundreds of dollars annually and drink cleaner water by installing a water filtration system at home and improving your tap (or well) water.

Shelter

Housing and all the costs associated with it (utilities, furniture, appliances, and, if you're a homeowner, maintenance, repairs, and home insurance) can consume a large portion of your monthly income. People often overlook opportunities to save money in this category.

_____

_____

_____

Reducing rental costs

Rent can take up a sizable chunk of your monthly take-home pay. Many people consider rent to be a fixed and inflexible part of their expenses, but it's not. Here's what you can do to cut down your rental costs:

- **Move to a lower-cost rental.** Of course, a lower-cost rental may not be as nice — it may be smaller, lack a private parking spot, or be located in a less popular area. Remember that the less you spend renting, the more you can save. Just be sure to factor in all the costs of a new location, including the possible higher commuting costs.

- **Share a rental.** Living alone has some benefits, but financially speaking, it's a luxury. If you rent a larger place with roommates, your rental costs should be a good deal less, and you'll get more home for your rental dollars.

- **Negotiate your rental increases.** Every year, like clockwork, your landlord bumps up your rent by a certain percentage. If your local rental market is soft or your living quarters are deteriorating, stand up for yourself! You have more leverage and power than you probably

t landlord doesn't want to lose good ten-
rent on time. Filling vacancies takes time
State your case: You've been a responsible
your research shows comparable rentals
going ...ess.

- **Buy rather than rent.** Purchasing your own place may
  seem costly, but in the long run, owning is cheaper than
  renting, and you have something to show for it in the
  end. If you purchase real estate with a 30-year fixed-rate
  mortgage, your mortgage payment (which is your biggest ownership expense) remains constant. Only your
  property taxes, maintenance, and insurance costs are
  exposed to the vagaries of inflation. As a renter, your
  entire monthly housing cost can rise with increases in
  the cost of living.

Reducing homeowner expenses

As every homeowner knows, houses suck up money. You
should be especially careful to watch your money in this area
of your budget.

- **Know what you can afford.** Whether you're on the
  verge of buying your first home or trading up to a
  more costly property, crunch some realistic numbers

before you commit. Calculate how much you can afford to spend monthly on a home. Do the exercises in Chapter 3, on saving for retirement, and Chapter 4, on where you're spending your money, to help you calculate the amount you can afford.

- **Rent out a room.** Because selling your home to buy a less expensive place can be a big hassle, consider taking in a tenant (or charge those adult "children" still living at home!) to reduce your housing expenses. Check out the renter thoroughly: Get references, run a credit report, research civil and criminal databases online, and talk about ground rules and expectations before sharing your space. Don't forget to check with your insurance company to see whether your homeowner's policy needs adjustments to cover potential liability from renting.

- **Refinance your mortgage.** Many people don't keep up-to-date on mortgage rates. If interest rates are lower than they were when you obtained your current mortgage, you may be able to save money by refinancing.

- **Appeal your property tax assessment.** If you bought your property when housing prices were higher in your area than they are now, you may be able to save money

_____

_____

_____

by appealing your assessment. Also, if you live in an area where your assessment is based on how the local assessor valued the property (rather than what you paid for your home), your home may be overassessed. Check with your local assessor's office for the appeals procedure you need to follow. An appraiser's recent evaluation of your property may help — you may already have one if you refinanced your mortgage recently. Also, review how the assessor valued your property compared with similar ones nearby — mistakes happen.

- **Reduce utility costs.** Sometimes you have to spend money to save money. Old refrigerators, for example, can waste a lot of electricity. Insulate to save on heating and air-conditioning bills. Install water flow regulators in shower heads. When planting your yard, don't select water-guzzling plants, and keep your lawn area reasonable.

Transportation costs

America is a car-driven society. In most other countries, cars are a luxury. If more people in the United States thought of cars as a luxury, Americans might have far fewer financial

_____

_____

_____

problems. Not only do cars pollute the air and clog the highways, but they also cost you a bundle.

Purchasing a quality car and using it wisely can reduce the cost of car ownership. Using alternative modes of transportation can also help you save.

Contrary to advertising slogans, cars aren't built to last; manufacturers don't want you to stick with the same car forever. New models are constantly introduced with new features and styling changes. But getting a new set of wheels every few years is an expensive luxury. Don't try to keep up with the Joneses as they show off their new cars every year. Let your neighbors admire you for your thriftiness and wisdom instead.

Research before you buy a car

When you buy a car, you don't just pay the initial sticker price: You also have to pay for gas, insurance, registration fees, maintenance, and repairs. You may also owe sales and/or personal property taxes. Don't simply compare sticker prices; think about the total, long-term costs of car ownership and see whether they fit into your budget while still allowing you to save toward your goals.

IntelliChoice (www.intellichoice.com) provides information about all categories of ownership costs, warranties, and dealer costs for new cars, which are rated based on total ownership costs. Edmunds (www.edmunds.com) provides more general information about different makes and models of both new and used cars. Please be aware that these sites have advertising and may receive referral fees if you buy a car through a dealer their website refers you to. *Consumer Reports'* annual car guide also has good information and data.

Buy your car with cash

The main reason people end up spending more than they can afford on a car is that they finance the purchase. As I discuss throughout this book, you should avoid borrowing money for consumption purchases, especially for items that depreciate in value (like cars). A car is most definitely *not* an investment.

Leasing is generally more expensive than borrowing money to buy a car. Leasing is like a long-term car rental. Everyone knows how well rental cars get treated — leased cars are treated just as well, which is one of the reasons leasing is so costly.

"But I can't buy a new car with cash," you may be thinking. Before you embrace that thought, consider the following:

- **If you lack sufficient cash to buy a new car, don't buy a new car!** Most of the world's population can't even afford a car, let alone a new one! Buy a car that you can afford — which for most people is a used one.

_____

_____

_____

- **Don't fall for the rationale that says buying a used car means lots of maintenance, repair expenses, and problems.** Do your homework and buy a good quality used car. A good used car costs less to buy and, thanks to lower insurance costs (and possibly property taxes), less to operate.

If you absolutely must finance a portion or all of your new car, and you are a homeowner, consider using a home equity line of credit. Interest on amounts of up to $100,000 of debt is currently tax deductible.

Buy commuter passes

In many areas, you can purchase train, bus, or subway passes to help reduce the cost of commuting. Many toll bridges also have booklets of tickets or passes that you can buy at a discount. Electronic passes like E-Z Pass help you keep moving through toll plazas and eliminate sitting in toll collection lines that waste your time and gas. Some areas even allow before-tax dollars to be withheld from your paycheck to buy commuter passes.

_____

_____

_____

Service your car regularly

Sure, servicing your car (for example, changing the oil every 5,000 miles) costs money, but it saves you dough in the long run by extending the operating life of your car. Servicing your car also reduces the chance that your car will conk out in the middle of nowhere, which requires a hefty towing charge to a service station. Stalling on the freeway during peak rush hour and having thousands of angry commuters stuck behind you is even worse.

Energy costs

Escalating energy prices remind all of us how much we depend on and use oil, electricity, and natural gas in our daily lives. A number of terrific websites are packed with suggestions and tips for how to lower your energy costs. Before I present those to you, however, here are the basics:

- **Drive fuel-efficient cars and drive efficiently.** If you're safety minded, you know how dangerous driving can be and aren't willing to risk your life driving a pint-size vehicle just to get 50 miles per gallon. That said, you can drive safe cars that are fuel-efficient.

- **Be thrifty at home.** Get all family members to turn off lights they don't need. Turn down the heat at night, which saves money and helps you sleep better, and turn it down when no one is home.

- **Service and maintain what you have.** Anything that uses energy — from your cars to your furnace — should be regularly serviced. For instance, make sure you replace your filters.

- **Investigate energy efficiency before you buy.** This advice applies not only to appliances but also to an entire home. Some builders are building energy efficiency into their new homes.

Clothing costs

Given the amount of money that some people spend on clothing and related accessories, I've come to believe that people in nudist colonies must be great savers! But you probably live among the clothed mainstream of society, so here's a short list of economical ideas:

- **Avoid clothing that requires dry cleaning.**
- **Don't chase the latest fashions.**
- **Minimize accessories.**

_____

_____

_____

Repaying your debt

In Chapter 7, I discuss strategies for reducing the cost of carrying consumer debt. The *best* way to reduce the costs of such debt is to avoid it in the first place when you're making consumption purchases.

You can avoid consumer debt by eliminating your access to credit or by limiting your purchase of consumer items to what you can pay off each month. Borrow only for long-term investments (see Chapter 2 for more information).

Don't keep a credit card that charges you an annual fee, especially if you pay your balance in full each month. Many no-fee credit cards exist — and some even offer you a benefit for using them:

- **Discover Card** (800-347-2683; www.discover.com) rebates up to 1 percent of purchases in cash.

- **Armed Forces Benefit Association (AFBA)/5Star Bank** (800-776-2265; www.afba.com) offers no-fee cards that accumulate points toward rewards such as airline tickets, merchandise, gift cards, or cash back.

_____

_____

_____

- **USAA Federal Savings** (800-922-9092; www.usaa.com) offers no-fee cards for members of the military and their immediate relatives.

Consider the cards in the preceding list only if you pay your balance in full each month because no-fee cards typically don't offer the lowest interest rates for balances carried month-to-month. The small rewards that you earn won't do you much good if they're negated by high interest charges.

Phone bills

Thanks to increased competition and technology, telephoning costs continue to fall. If you haven't looked for lower rates in recent years, you're probably paying more than you need to for quality phone service. Unfortunately, shopping among the many service providers is difficult. Plans come with different restrictions, minimums, and bells and whistles.

You may have to switch companies to reduce your bill, but many people can save significantly with their current phone company simply by getting onto a better calling plan. So before you spend hours shopping around, contact your current local and long-distance providers and ask them which of their calling plans offer the lowest cost for you based on your usage.

Cellphones are ubiquitous. Every cellphone carrier offers its own service plans, and those plans change frequently. Shop around and do your best to compare plans and rates to get the best deal. Break a multi-line plan into the cost per line for an easier comparison between carriers.

Technology

Americans today have email, cellphones, smartphones, voice-mail, tablets, satellite TV, the Internet, and too many other ways to stay in touch and entertained 24/7. Visit a store that sells electronics, and you'll find no end to new gadgets.

These technologies can have a detrimental impact on people's lives. As it is, most families struggle to find quality time together given their work obligations, long school days, and various other activities. At home, all these technology choices compete for attention and often pull families apart. The cost for all these services and gadgets adds up, leading to continued enslavement to your job. Err on the side of keeping your

_____

_____

_____

life simple. Doing so costs less, reduces stress, and allows more time for the things that really do matter in life.

The worst way to shop for electronics and technology-based products is to wander around stores selling lots of these goods while a salesperson pitches you things. Educate yourself (check out *Consumer Reports* and CNET's website at www.cnet.com) and determine what you really need instead of going to a store and being seduced by a salesperson.

Medical expenses

The cost of healthcare continues to go up. Your health insurance probably covers most of your healthcare needs, but many plans require you to pay for certain expenses out of your own pocket.

Medical care and supplies are like any other services and products — prices and quality vary. And medicine in the United States is a business. A conflict of interest exists whenever the person recommending treatment benefits financially from providing that treatment. Many studies have documented some of the unnecessary surgeries and medical procedures that have resulted from this conflict of interest.

Remember to shop around when seeking health insurance. Don't take any one physician's advice as gospel. Always get a second opinion for any major surgery. Most health insurance plans, out of economic self-interest, require a second opinion anyway.

Alternative medicine (holistic, for example) is gaining attention because of its focus on preventive care and the treatment of the whole body or person. Although alternative medicine can be dangerous if you're in critical condition, alternative treatment for some forms of chronic pain or disease may be worth investigating. Alternative medicine may lead to better *and* lower-cost healthcare.

If you have to take certain drugs on an ongoing basis and pay for them out-of-pocket, ordering through a mail-order company can bring down your costs and help make refilling your prescriptions more convenient. Ask your health plan provider for more information about this option. Also inquire about generic versions of drugs.

8

Debt

Accumulating *bad debt* (consumer debt) by buying things like new living room furniture or a new car that you really can't afford is like living on a diet of sugar and caffeine: a quick fix with little nutritional value. Borrowing on your credit card for short-term pleasures is detrimental to your long-term financial health.

When you use debt for investing in your future, I call it *good debt* (see Chapter 2). Borrowing money to pay for an education, to buy real estate, or to invest in a small business is like eating fruits and vegetables for their vitamins. That's not to say that you can't get yourself into trouble when using good debt. Just as you can gorge yourself on too much good food, you can develop financial indigestion from too much good debt.

In this chapter, I help you battle the pervasive problem of consumer debt. Getting rid of your bad debts may be even more difficult than giving up junk food. But in the long run, you'll be glad you did; you'll be financially healthier and emotionally happier. And after you get rid of your high-cost consumer debts, make sure you practice the best way to avoid future credit problems: *Don't borrow with bad debt.*

Before you decide which debt reduction strategies make sense for you, you must first consider your overall financial situation (see Chapter 2) and assess your alternatives. (I discuss strategies for reducing your current spending — which help you free up more cash to pay down your debts — in Chapter 7.)

Using Savings to Reduce Your Consumer Debt

Many people build a mental brick wall between their savings and investment accounts and their consumer debt accounts. By failing to view their finances holistically, they fall into the habit of looking at these accounts individually. The thought of putting a door in that big brick wall doesn't occur to them. This section helps you see how your savings can be used to lower your consumer debt.

How you gain

If you have the savings to pay off consumer debt, like high-interest credit card and auto loans, consider doing so. (Make sure you pay off the loans with the highest interest rates first.) Sure, you diminish your savings, but you also reduce your debts. Although your savings and investments may be earning decent returns, the interest you're paying on your consumer debts is likely higher.

Paying off consumer loans on a credit card at, say, 12 percent is like finding an investment with a guaranteed return of 12 percent — *tax free*. You would actually need to find an investment that yielded even more — around 18 percent — to net 12 percent after paying taxes on those investment returns in order to justify not paying off your 12 percent loans. The higher your tax bracket (see Chapter 10), the higher the return you need on your investments to justify keeping high-interest consumer debt.

Even if you think you're an investing genius and you can earn more on your investments, pay down your consumer debts anyway. To chase that higher potential return from investments, you need to take substantial risk. You *may* earn more investing in that hot stock tip or that bargain real estate, but you probably won't.

_____

_____

_____

If you use your savings to pay down consumer debts, be careful to leave yourself enough of an emergency cushion. (In Chapter 3, I tell you how to determine what size emergency reserve you should have.) You want to be in a position to withstand an unexpected large expense or temporary loss of income. On the other hand, if you use savings to pay down credit card debt, you can run your credit card balances back up in a financial pinch (unless your card gets canceled), or you can turn to a family member or friend for a low-interest loan.

Finding the funds to pay down debts

Have you ever reached into the pocket of an old winter parka and found a rolled-up $20 bill you forgot you had? Stumbling across some forgotten funds is always a pleasant experience. But before you root through all of your closets in search of stray cash to help you pay down that nagging credit card debt, check out some of these financial jacket pockets you may have overlooked:

_____

_____

_____

- **Borrow against your cash value life insurance policy.** If a life insurance agent ever lured you into buying a policy, she probably sold you a cash value policy because it pays high commissions to insurance agents. Or perhaps your parents bought one of these policies for you when you were a child. Borrow against the cash value to pay down your debts.

- **Sell investments held outside of retirement accounts.** Maybe you have some shares of stock or a Treasury bond gathering dust in your safety deposit box. Consider cashing in these investments to pay down your consumer loans. Just be sure to consider the tax consequences of selling these investments. If possible, sell only those investments that won't generate a big tax bill.

- **Tap the equity in your home.** If you're a homeowner, you may be able to tap in to your home's *equity*, which is the difference between the property's market value and the outstanding loan balance. You can generally borrow against real estate at a lower interest rate and get a tax deduction. However, you must take care to

ensure that you don't overborrow on your home and
risk losing it to foreclosure.

- **Borrow against your employer's retirement account.**
  Check with your employer's benefits department to
  see whether you can borrow against your retirement
  account balance. The interest rate is usually reasonable.
  Be careful, though — if you leave or lose your job, you
  may have to repay the loan within 60 days. Also recognize that you'll miss out on investment returns on the
  money borrowed.

- **Lean on family.** They know you, love you, realize your
  shortcomings, and probably won't be as cold-hearted as
  some bankers. Money borrowed from family members
  can have strings attached, of course. Treating the obliga-
  tion seriously is important. To avoid misunderstand-
  ings, write up a simple agreement listing the terms and
  conditions of the loan. Unless your family members
  are the worst bankers on the planet, you'll probably
  get a fair interest rate, and your family will have the
  satisfaction of helping you out. Just don't forget to pay
  them back.

Decreasing Debt When You Lack Savings

If you lack savings to throw at your consumer debts, you have some work to do. If you're spending all of your income, you need to figure out how you can decrease your spending (see Chapter 7) and/or increase your income. In the meantime, you need to slow the growth of your debt.

Reduce your credit card's interest rate

Different credit cards charge different interest rates. So why pay 14, 16, or 18 percent (or more) when you can pay less? The credit card business is highly competitive. Until you get your debt paid off, slow the growth of your debt by reducing the interest rate you're paying. Here are sound ways to do that:

- **Apply for a lower-rate credit card.** If you're earning a decent income, you're not too burdened with debt, and you have a clean credit record, qualifying for lower-rate cards is relatively painless. Some persistence (and cleanup work) may be required if you have income and debt problems or nicks in your credit report.

After you're approved for a new, lower-interest-rate card, you can simply transfer your outstanding balance from your higher-rate card.

CreditCards.com's website (www.creditcards.com) carries information on low-interest-rate and no-annual-fee cards (among others, including secured cards).

- **Call the bank(s) that issued your current high-interest-rate credit card(s) and tell them you want to cancel your card(s) because you found a competitor that offers no annual fee and a lower interest rate.** Your bank may choose to match the terms of the "competitor" rather than lose you as a customer. But be careful with this strategy and consider paying off or transferring the balance. Canceling the credit card, especially if it's one you've had for several years, may lower your credit score.

- **While you're paying down your credit card balance(s), stop making new charges on cards that have outstanding balances.** Many people don't realize that interest starts to accumulate *immediately* when they carry a balance. *You have no grace period* — the 20 or so days you normally have to pay your balance in full without incurring interest charges — if you carry a credit card balance from month to month.

Credit-card terms and conditions

Avoid getting lured into applying for a credit card that hypes an extremely low interest rate. One such card advertised a 1.9 percent rate, but you had to dig into the fine print for the rest of the story.

First, any card that offers such a low interest rate will honor that rate only for a short period of time — in this case, six months. After six months, the interest rate skyrocketed to nearly 15 percent.

Additionally, make just one late payment or exceed your credit limit, and the company raises your interest rate to 19.8 percent (or even 24 percent, 29 percent, or more) and levies a $25 fee — $35 thereafter. If you want a cash advance on your card, you get charged a fee equal to 3 percent of the amount advanced. (Some banks have even advertised 0 percent interest rates — although that rate generally has applied only to balances transferred from another card, and such cards have been subject to all of the other vagaries discussed in this section.)

I'm not saying that everyone should avoid this type of card. Such a card may make sense for you if you want to transfer an outstanding balance and then pay off that balance within a few months and cancel the card to avoid getting socked with the card's high fees.

_____

_____

_____

If you hunt around for a low-interest-rate credit card, be sure to check out all the terms and conditions. Start by reviewing the uniform rates and terms disclosure, which details the myriad fees and conditions (especially how much your interest rate can increase for missed or late payments). Also, be sure you understand how the future interest rate is determined on cards that charge variable interest rates.

Cut up your credit cards

If you tend to live beyond your means by buying on credit, get rid of the culprit — the credit card. To kick the habit, a smoker needs to toss *all* the cigarettes, and an alcoholic needs to get rid of *all* the booze. Cut up *all* of your credit cards and call the card issuers to cancel your accounts. And when you buy consumer items such as cars and furniture, do not apply for E-Z credit.

Just a couple generations ago, credit cards didn't even exist. People paid with cash and checks — imagine that! You *can* function without buying anything on a credit card. In certain cases, you may need a card as collateral — such as when renting a car. When you bring back the rental car, however, you can pay with cash or a check. Leave the card at home in the back of your sock drawer or freezer, and pull (or thaw) it out only for the occasional car rental.

If you can trust yourself, keep a separate credit card *only* for new purchases that you know you can absolutely pay in full each month. No one needs three, five, or ten credit cards. You can live with one, given the wide acceptance of most cards.

Retailers such as department stores and gas stations just love to issue cards. Not only do these cards charge outrageously high interest rates, but they're also not widely accepted like Visa and MasterCard. Virtually all retailers accept Visa and MasterCard. More credit lines mean more temptation to spend what you can't afford.

If you decide to keep one widely accepted credit card instead of getting rid of them all, be careful. You may be tempted to let debt accumulate and roll over for a month or two, starting the whole horrible process of running up your consumer debt again. Rather than keeping one credit card, consider getting a debit card.

Use debit cards

Credit cards are the main reason today's consumers are buying more than they can afford. So logic says that one way you can keep your spending in check is to stop using your credit cards. But in a society that's used to handing over MasterCard and Visa credit cards for purchases, changing habits is hard. And you may be concerned that carrying your checkbook or cash can be a hassle or can be costly if you're mugged.

Debit cards offer the best of both worlds. The beauty of the debit card is that it offers you the convenience of making purchases with a piece of plastic without the temptation or ability to run up credit card debt. Debit cards keep you from spending money you don't have and help you live within your means.

A *debit card* looks just like a credit card with either the Visa or MasterCard logo. The big difference between debit cards and credit cards is that debit card purchase amounts are deducted electronically from your checking account within days.

If you switch to a debit card and you keep your checking account balance low and don't ordinarily balance your checkbook, you may need to start balancing it. Otherwise, you may face charges for overdrawing your account.

Here are some other differences between debit and credit cards:

- If you pay your credit card bill in full and on time each month, your credit card gives you free use of the money you owe until it's time to pay the bill. Debit cards take the money out of your checking account almost immediately.

- Credit cards make it easier for you to dispute charges for problematic merchandise through the issuing bank. Most banks allow you to dispute charges for up to 60 days after purchase and will credit the disputed amount to your account pending resolution. Most debit cards offer a much shorter window, typically less than one week, for making disputes.

Because moving your checking account can be a hassle, see whether your current bank offers Visa or MasterCard debit cards. If your bank doesn't offer one, shop among the major banks in your area, which are likely to offer the cards. Because such cards come with checking accounts, make sure you do some comparison shopping among the different account features and fees.

_____

_____

_____

Credit Counseling Agencies

Before the passage of the 2005 bankruptcy laws (see Chapter 9), each year hundreds of thousands of debt-burdened consumers sought "counseling" from credit counseling service offices. Now, more than a million people annually get the required counseling. Unfortunately, some people find that the service doesn't always work the way it's pitched.

Beware biased advice

Leona Davis, whose family racked up significant debt due largely to unexpected medical expenses and a reduction in her income, found herself in trouble with too much debt. So she turned to one of the large, nationally promoted credit counseling services, which she heard about through its advertising and marketing materials.

The credit counseling agency Davis went to markets itself as a "nonprofit community service." Davis, like many others, found that the "service" was not objective. After her experience, Davis feels that a more appropriate name for the organization she worked with would be the Credit Card Collection Agency.

Unbeknownst to Davis and most of the other people who use supposed credit counseling agencies is the fact that the vast majority of their funding comes from the fees that creditors pay them. Most credit counseling agencies collect fees on a commission basis — just as collection agencies do! Their strategy is to place those who come in for help on their "debt management program." Under this program, counselees like Davis agree to pay a certain amount per month to the agency, which in turn parcels out the money to the various creditors.

Because of Davis's tremendous outstanding consumer debt (it exceeded her annual income), her repayment plan was doomed to failure. Davis managed to make 10 months' worth of payments, largely because she raided a retirement account for $28,000. Had Davis filed bankruptcy (which she ultimately needed to do), she would've been able to keep her retirement money. But Davis's counselor never discussed the bankruptcy option. "I received no counseling," says Davis. "Real counselors take the time to understand your situation and offer options. I was offered one solution: a forced payment plan."

Others who have consulted various credit counseling agencies confirm that some agencies use a cookie-cutter approach to dealing with debt. Such agencies typically recommend that debtors go on a repayment plan that has the consumer pay, say, 3 percent of each outstanding loan balance to the agency, which in turn pays the money to creditors.

Unable to keep up with the enormous monthly payments, Davis finally turned to an attorney and filed for bankruptcy — but not before she had unnecessarily lost thousands of dollars because of the biased recommendations.

Although credit counseling agencies' promotional materials and counselors aren't shy about highlighting the drawbacks to bankruptcy, counselors are reluctant to discuss the negative impact of signing up for a debt payment plan. Davis's counselor never told her that restructuring her credit card payments would tarnish her credit reports and scores.

If you're considering bankruptcy or are otherwise unable to meet your current debt obligations, be sure to read Chapter 9. Then interview any counseling agency you may be considering working with. Remember that you're the customer and you should do your homework first and be in control. Don't allow anyone or any agency to make you feel that they're in a position of power simply because of your financial troubles.

Ask questions and avoid debt management programs

Probably the most important question to ask a counseling agency is whether it offers *debt management programs* (DMPs), whereby you're put on a repayment plan with your creditors and the agency gets a monthly fee for handling the payments. You do *not* want to work with an agency offering DMPs because of conflicts of interest. An agency can't offer objective advice about all your options for dealing with debt, including bankruptcy, if it has a financial incentive to put you on a DMP.

 The Institute for Financial Literacy is a good agency that doesn't offer DMPs (866-662-4932; www.financiallit.org).

Here are some additional questions that the Federal Trade Commission suggests you ask prospective counseling agencies you may hire:

- **What are your fees? Are there setup and/or monthly fees?** Get a specific price quote in writing.

- **What if I can't afford to pay your fees or make contributions?** If an organization won't help you because you can't afford to pay, look elsewhere for help.

- **Will I have a formal written agreement or contract with you?** Don't sign anything without reading it first. Make sure all verbal promises are in writing.

- **Are you licensed to offer your services in my state?** You should work only with a licensed agency.

- **What are the qualifications of your counselors? Are they accredited or certified by an outside organization? If so, by whom? If not, how are they trained?** Try to use an organization whose counselors are trained by a nonaffiliated party.

- **What assurance do I have that information about me (including my address, phone number, and financial information) will be kept confidential and secure?** A reputable agency can provide you with a clearly written privacy policy.

- **How are your employees compensated? Are they paid more if I sign up for certain services, if I pay a fee, or if I make a contribution to your organization?** Employees who work on an incentive basis are less likely to have your best interests in mind than those who earn a straight salary that isn't influenced by your choices.

_____

_____

_____

Stopping the Spending Cycle

Regardless of how you deal with paying off your debt, you're in real danger of falling back into old habits. Backsliding happens to people who file bankruptcy and those who use savings or home equity to eliminate their debt. This section speaks to that risk and tells you what to do about it.

Resist the credit temptation

Getting out of debt can be challenging, but I have confidence that you can do it with this book by your side. In addition to the ideas I discuss earlier in this chapter (such as eliminating all your credit cards and getting a debit card), the following list provides some additional tactics you can use to limit the influence credit cards hold over your life. (If you're concerned about the impact that any of these tactics may have on your credit rating, please see Chapter 2.)

- **Reduce your credit limit.** If you choose not to get rid of all your credit cards or get a debit card, be sure to keep a lid on your credit card's *credit limit* (the maximum balance allowed on your card). You don't have to accept the increase just because your bank keeps raising your credit limit to reward you for being such a profitable customer. Call your credit card service's toll-free phone number and lower your credit limit to a level you're comfortable with.

- **Replace your credit card with a charge card.** A charge card (such as the American Express Card) requires you to pay your balance in full each billing period. You have no credit line or interest charges. Of course, spending more than you can afford to pay when the bill comes due is possible. But you'll be much less likely to over-spend if you know you have to pay in full monthly.

- **Never buy anything on credit that depreciates in value.** Meals out, cars, clothing, and shoes all depreci-ate in value. Don't buy these things on credit. Borrow money only for sound investments — education, real estate, or your own business, for example.

- **Think in terms of total cost.** Everything sounds cheaper in terms of monthly payments — that's how salespeople entice you into buying things you can't afford. Use the calculator on your smartphone to tally up the sticker price, interest charges, and upkeep. The total cost will scare you. It should.

_____

_____

_____

- **Stop the junk mail avalanche.** Look at your daily mail — half of it is probably solicitations and mail order catalogs. You can save some trees and some time sorting junk mail by removing yourself from most mailing lists. To remove your name from mailing lists, contact the Direct Marketing Association (you can register through its website at www.dmachoice.org or call 212-768-7277 between 9 a.m. and 2 p.m. Eastern Standard Time, Monday through Thursday).

  To remove your name from the major credit reporting agency lists that are used by credit card solicitation companies, call 888-567-8688. Also, tell any credit card companies you keep cards with that you want your account marked to indicate you don't want any of your personal information shared with telemarketing firms.

- **Limit what you can spend.** Go shopping with a small amount of cash and no plastic or checks. That way, you can spend only what little cash you have with you.

_____

_____

_____

Identify a compulsion

No matter how hard they try to break the habit, some people become addicted to spending and accumulating debt. It becomes a chronic problem that starts to interfere with other aspects of their lives and can lead to problems at work and with family and friends.

Debtors Anonymous (DA) is a nonprofit organization that provides support (primarily through group meetings) to people trying to break their debt accumulation and spending habits. DA is modeled after the 12-step Alcoholics Anonymous (AA) program.

Like AA, Debtors Anonymous works with people from all walks of life and socioeconomic backgrounds. You can find people who are financially on the edge, $100,000-plus income earners, and everybody in between at DA meetings. Even former millionaires join the program.

DA has a simple questionnaire that helps determine whether you're a problem debtor. If you answer "yes" to at least 8 of the following 15 questions, you may be developing or already have a compulsive spending and debt accumulation habit:

_____

_____

_____

- Are your debts making your home life unhappy?

- Does the pressure of your debts distract you from your daily work?

- Are your debts affecting your reputation?

- Do your debts cause you to think less of yourself?

- Have you ever given false information to obtain credit?

- Have you ever made unrealistic promises to your creditors?

- Does the pressure of your debts make you careless when it comes to the welfare of your family?

- Do you ever fear that your employer, family, or friends will learn the extent of your total indebtedness?

- When faced with a difficult financial situation, does the prospect of borrowing give you an inordinate feeling of relief?

- Does the pressure of your debts cause you to have difficulty sleeping?

- Has the pressure of your debts ever caused you to consider getting drunk?

_____

_____

_____

- Have you ever borrowed money without giving adequate consideration to the rate of interest you're required to pay?

- Do you usually expect a negative response when you're subject to a credit investigation?

- Have you ever developed a strict regimen for paying off your debts, only to break it under pressure?

- Do you justify your debts by telling yourself that you are superior to the "other" people, and when you get your "break," you'll be out of debt?

To find a Debtors Anonymous (DA) support group in your area, visit the DA website at www. debtorsanonymous.org or contact the DA's national headquarters by phone at 800-421-2383 or 781-453-2743.

9

Filing Bankruptcy

For consumers in over their heads with their debt, the realization that their monthly income is increasingly exceeded by their bill payments is usually a traumatic one. In many cases, years can pass before people consider a drastic measure like filing bankruptcy. Both financial and emotional issues come into play in one of the most difficult and painful, yet potentially beneficial, decisions.

This chapter explains the benefits and drawbacks of filing for bankruptcy, provides an overview of bankruptcy laws, details the differences between Chapter 7 and 13 bankruptcy, and points you to resources for advice.

Bankruptcy Benefits

Bankruptcy allows certain types of debts to be completely eliminated or *discharged*. Debts that typically can be discharged include credit card, medical, auto, utilities, and rent.

Debts that may *not* be canceled generally include child support, alimony, student loans, taxes, and court-ordered damages (for example, drunk driving settlements). When the ratio of high-interest consumer debt relative to annual income exceeds 25 percent, filing bankruptcy may be your best option.

Eliminating your debt also allows you to start working toward your financial goals. Depending on the amount of debt you have outstanding relative to your income, you may need a decade or more to pay it all off.

Filing bankruptcy offers not only financial benefits but emotional benefits, as well. Many people are happy to be free from the debts and are relieved when the collection calls stop.

Bankruptcy Drawbacks

Filing bankruptcy, needless to say, has a number of drawbacks. First, bankruptcy appears on your credit report for up to ten years, so you'll have difficulty obtaining credit, especially in the years immediately following your filing. However, if you already have problems on your credit report (because of late payments or a failure to pay previous debts), the damage has already been done. And without savings, you're probably not going to be making major purchases (such as a home) in the next several years anyway.

If you do file bankruptcy, getting credit in the future is still possible. You may be able to obtain a *secured credit card*, which requires you to deposit money in a bank account equal to the credit limit on your credit card. Of course, you'll be better off without the temptation of any credit cards and better served with a debit card. Also, know that if you can hold down a stable job, most creditors will be willing to give you loans within a few years of your filing bankruptcy. Almost all lenders ignore bankruptcy after five to seven years.

Another drawback of bankruptcy is that it costs money, and those expenses have jumped higher due to the requirements of bankruptcy laws (see the following section). Court filing and legal fees can easily exceed $1,000, especially in higher cost-of-living areas.

And finally, most people find that filing bankruptcy causes emotional stress. Admitting that your personal income can't keep pace with your debt obligations is painful. Although filing bankruptcy clears the decks of debt and gives you a fresh financial start, feeling a profound sense of failure (and sometimes shame) is common. Despite the increasing incidence of bankruptcy, bankruptcy filers are reluctant to talk about it with others, including family and friends.

Another part of the emotional side of filing bankruptcy is that you must open your personal financial affairs to court scrutiny and court control during the several months it takes to administer a bankruptcy. A court-appointed bankruptcy trustee oversees your case and tries to recover as much of your property as possible to satisfy the *creditors* — those to whom you owe money.

Some people also feel that they're shirking responsibility by filing for bankruptcy. One client I worked with should have filed, but she couldn't bring herself to do it. She said, "I spent that money, and it's my responsibility to pay it back."

If you file for bankruptcy, don't feel bad about not paying back the bank. Credit cards are one of the most profitable lines of business for banks. The nice merchants from whom you bought the merchandise have already been paid. *Charge-offs* — the banker's term for taking the loss on debt that you discharge through bankruptcy — are the banker's cost, which is another reason why the interest rate is so high on credit cards and why borrowing on them is a bad idea.

Bankruptcy Laws

The Bankruptcy Abuse and Prevention Act of 2005 has had a significant effect on consumers who are considering filing for bankruptcy. Major creditors, such as credit card companies, lobbied heavily for laws. Although they didn't get everything they wanted, they got a lot, which doesn't benefit those folks in dire financial condition contemplating bankruptcy. Don't despair, though; help and information can overcome the worst provisions of this law. Here are the major elements of the personal bankruptcy laws:

- **Required counseling:** Before filing for bankruptcy, individuals must complete credit counseling, the purpose of which is to explore your options for dealing with debt, including (but not limited to) bankruptcy and developing a debt repayment plan. (Chapter 7 explains how to pick a top-notch counseling agency.)

  To have debts discharged through bankruptcy, the law requires a second type of counseling called "Debtor Education." All credit counseling and debtor education must be completed by an approved organization on the U.S. Trustee's website (www.justice.gov/ust). Click on the link Credit Counseling & Debtor Education.

- **Means testing:** Some high-income earners may be precluded from filing the form of bankruptcy that actually discharges debts (called Chapter 7) and instead be forced to use the form of bankruptcy that involves a repayment plan (called Chapter 13).

- **Increased requirements placed on filers and attorneys:** The means testing alone has created a good deal of additional work for bankruptcy filers, work generally done by attorneys. Filers, including lawyers, must also attest to the accuracy of submitted information, which has attorneys doing more verification work. Thus, it's no surprise that when the bankruptcy laws were passed, legal fees increased significantly — jumps of 30 to 40 percent were common.

- **New rules for people who recently moved:** Individual states have their own provisions for how much personal property and home equity you can keep. Before the passage of the 2005 laws, shortly before filing bankruptcy, people moved to a state that allowed them to keep more. Under the law, you must live in the state for at least two years before filing bankruptcy in that state and using that state's personal property exemptions. To use a given state's *homestead exemption*, which dictates how much home equity you may protect, you must have lived in that state for at least 40 months.

Chapter 7 and Chapter 13 Bankruptcy

You can file one of two forms of personal bankruptcy: Chapter 7 or Chapter 13. Here are the essentials regarding each type:

- **Chapter 7 allows you to discharge, or cancel, certain debts.** This form of bankruptcy makes the most sense when you have significant debts that you're legally allowed to cancel. (See "Bankruptcy Benefits" earlier in this chapter for details on which debts can be canceled, or discharged.)

- **Chapter 13 comes up with a repayment schedule that requires you to pay your debts over several years.** Chapter 13 stays on your credit record (just like Chapter 7), *but it doesn't eliminate debt,* so its value is limited — usually to dealing with debts like taxes that can't be discharged through bankruptcy. Chapter 13 can keep creditors at bay until you work out a repayment schedule in the courts.

_____

_____

_____

Seeking Bankruptcy Advice

If you want to find out more about the pros, cons, and details of filing for bankruptcy, pick up a copy of *The New Bankruptcy: Will It Work for You?* by attorneys Leon Bayer and Stephen R. Elias (Nolo Press). If you're comfortable with your decision to file and you think you can complete the paperwork, check out *How to File for Chapter 7 Bankruptcy*, by attorneys Stephen R. Elias and Albin Renauer (Nolo Press), which comes with all the necessary filing forms.

Hiring a paralegal typing service to prepare the forms, which can be a cost-effective way to get help with the process if you don't need heavy-duty legal advice, is an intermediate approach. To find a paralegal typing service in your area, enter "Paralegals" and your city's name in your favorite search engine.

10

Taxes

You pay a lot of money in taxes — probably more than you realize. Few people know just how much they pay in taxes each year. Most people remember whether they received a refund or owed money on their return. But when you file your tax return, all you're doing is settling up with tax authorities over the amount of taxes you paid during the year versus the total tax you owe based on your income and deductions.

The Taxes You Pay

Some people feel lucky when they get a refund, but all a refund really indicates is that you overpaid in taxes during the year.

You should have had this money in your own account all along. If you're consistently getting big refunds, you need to pay less tax throughout the year. (Fill out a W-4 to determine how much you should be paying in taxes throughout the year. You can obtain a W-4 through your employer's payroll department. If you're self-employed, you can obtain Form 1040-ES by calling the IRS at 800-TAX-FORM [800-829-3676] or visiting its website at www.irs.gov. The IRS website also has a helpful withholding calculator at www.irs.gov/Individuals/IRS-Withholding-Calculator.)

Instead of focusing on whether you're going to get a refund when you complete your annual tax return, concentrate on the *total* taxes you pay, which I discuss in the following section.

Your total taxes

To find out the *total* taxes you pay, you need to get out your federal and state tax returns. On each of those returns is a line that shows the *total tax you owed for the year:* This is Line 63 on the most recent federal 1040 returns. If you add up the totals from your federal and state income tax returns, you'll probably see one of your largest expenses.

The goal of this chapter is to help you legally and permanently reduce your total taxes. Understanding the tax system is the key to reducing your tax burden — if you don't, you'll surely pay more taxes than necessary. Your tax ignorance can lead to mistakes, which can be costly if the IRS and state government catch your underpayment errors. With the proliferation of computerized information and data tracking, discovering mistakes has never been easier.

The tax system, like other public policy, is built around incentives to encourage desirable behavior and activity. For example, saving for retirement is considered desirable because it encourages people to prepare for a time in their lives when they may be less able or interested in working so much and when they may have additional healthcare expenses. Therefore, the tax code offers all sorts of tax perks, which I discuss later in this chapter, to encourage people to save in retirement accounts.

You should make choices that work best for your life and situation. However, keep in mind that the *fewer* desirable activities you engage in, the more you will generally pay in taxes. If you understand the options, you can choose the ones that meet your needs as you approach different stages of your financial life.

_____

_____

_____

Your marginal tax rate

When it comes to taxes, *not all income is treated equally*. This fact is far from self-evident. If you work for an employer and earn a constant salary during the course of a year, a steady and equal amount of federal and state taxes is deducted from each paycheck. Thus, it appears as though all that earned income is being taxed equally.

In reality, however, you pay less tax on your first dollars of earnings and more tax on your *last* dollars of earnings. For example, if you're single and your taxable income (see the next section) totals $45,000 during 2017, you pay federal tax at the rate of 10 percent on the first $9,325 of taxable income, 15 percent on income between $9,326 and $37,950, and 25 percent on income from $37,951 up to $45,000.

Table 10-1 gives federal tax rates for singles and married households filing jointly.

Your *marginal tax rate* is the rate of tax you pay on your *last*, or so-called *highest*, dollars of income. A single person with taxable income of $45,000 has a federal marginal tax rate of 25 percent. In other words, she effectively pays 25 percent federal tax on her last dollars of income — those dollars in excess of $37,951.

Singles Taxable Income	Married-Filing-Jointly Taxable Income	Federal Tax Rate (Bracket)
$0–$9,325	$0–$18,650	10%
$9,326–$37,950	$18,651–$75,900	15%
$37,951–$91,900	$75,901–$153,100	25%
$91,901–$191,650	$153,101–$233,350	28%
$191,651–$416,700	$233,351–$416,700	33%
$416,701–$418,400	$416,701–$470,700	35%
More than $418,400	More than $470,700	39.6%

Table 10-1: *2017 Federal Income Tax Brackets and Rates*

Marginal tax rates are a powerful concept. Your marginal tax rate allows you to quickly calculate the additional taxes you'd have to pay on additional income. Conversely, you can enjoy quantifying the amount of taxes you save by reducing your taxable income, either by decreasing your income or by increasing your deductions.

As you're probably already painfully aware, you pay not only federal income taxes but also state income taxes — that is, unless you live in one of the handful of states (Alaska, Florida, Nevada, South Dakota, Texas, Washington, or Wyoming) that have no state income tax.

Your *total marginal rate* includes your federal *and* state tax rates (not to mention local income tax rates in the municipalities that have them).

 You can look up your state tax rate in your current state income tax preparation booklet.

Taxable income

Taxable income is the amount of income on which you pay income taxes. (In the sections that follow, I explain strategies for reducing your taxable income.) The following reasons explain why you don't pay taxes on your total income:

- **Not all income is taxable.** For example, you pay federal tax on the interest you earn on a bank savings account but not on the interest you earn from municipal bonds. Some income, such as from stock dividends and long-term capital gains, is taxed at lower rates.

- **You get to subtract deductions from your income.** Some deductions are available just for being a living, breathing human being. In 2017, single people get an automatic $6,350 standard deduction, and married couples filing jointly get $12,700. (People over age 65 and those who are blind get a slightly higher deduction.) Other expenses, such as mortgage interest and property taxes, are deductible in the event that these so-called itemized deductions exceed the standard deductions. When you contribute to qualified retirement plans, you also effectively get a deduction.

Employment Income Taxes

You're supposed to pay taxes on income you earn from work. Countless illegal methods can reduce your taxable employment income — for example, not reporting it — but if you use them, you can very well end up paying a heap of penalties and extra interest charges on top of the taxes you owe. And you may even get tossed in jail. Because I don't want you to serve jail time or lose even more money by paying unnecessary penalties and interest, this section focuses on the best *legal* ways to reduce your income taxes on your earnings from work.

Retirement plans

A retirement plan is one of the few relatively painless and authorized ways to reduce your taxable employment income. Besides reducing your taxes, retirement plans help you build a nest egg so you don't have to work for the rest of your life.

You can exclude money from your taxable income by tucking it away in employer-based retirement plans, such as 401(k) or 403(b) accounts, or self-employed retirement plans, such as SEP-IRAs. If your combined federal and state marginal tax rate is, say, 33 percent and you contribute $1,000 to one of these plans, you reduce your federal and state taxes by $330. Contribute another $1,000, and your taxes drop *another* $330 (as long as you're still in the same marginal tax rate). And when your money is inside a retirement account, it can compound and grow without taxation.

Many people miss this great opportunity to reduce their taxes because they *spend* all (or too much) of their current employment income and, therefore, have nothing (or little) left to put into a retirement account. If you're in this predicament, you first need to reduce your spending before you can contribute money to a retirement plan. (Chapter 7 explains how to decrease your spending.)

_____

_____

_____

If your employer doesn't offer the option of saving money through a retirement plan, lobby the benefits and human resources departments. If they resist, you may want to add this to your list of reasons for considering another employer. Many employers offer this valuable benefit, but some don't. Some company decision-makers either don't understand the value of these accounts or believe that they're too costly to set up and administer.

If your employer doesn't offer a retirement savings plan, individual retirement account (IRA) contributions may or may not be tax deductible, depending on your circumstances. You should first maximize contributions to the previously mentioned tax-deductible accounts.

Shifting some income

Income shifting is a tax-reduction technique that's an option only to those who can control *when* they receive their income.

For example, suppose your employer tells you in late December that you're eligible for a bonus. You're offered the option to receive your bonus in either December or January. If you're pretty certain that you'll be in a higher tax bracket next year, you should choose to receive your bonus in December.

_____

_____

_____

Or, suppose you run your own business and you think you'll be in a lower tax bracket next year. Perhaps you plan to take time off to be with a newborn or take an extended trip. You can send out some invoices later in the year so your customers won't pay you until January, which falls in the next tax year.

Deductions

Deductions are amounts you subtract from your adjusted gross income before calculating the tax you owe. To make things more complicated, the IRS gives you two methods for determining your total deductions. The good news is that you get to pick the method that leads to greater deductions — and hence, lower taxes. This section explains your options.

Standard versus itemized deductions

The first method for figuring deductions requires no thinking or calculating. If you have a relatively uncomplicated financial life, taking the *standard deduction* is generally the better option.

Single folks qualify for a $6,350 standard deduction, and married couples filing jointly get a $12,700 standard deduction in 2017. If you're 65 or older, or blind, you get a slightly higher standard deduction.

Itemizing your deductions on your tax return is the other method for determining your allowable deductions. This method is definitely more of a hassle, but if you can tally up more than the standard amounts, itemizing will save you money. Use Schedule A of IRS Form 1040 to sum up your itemized deductions.

Even if you take the standard deduction, take the time to peruse all the line items on Schedule A to familiarize yourself with the many legal itemized deductions. Figure out what's possible to deduct so you can make more-informed financial decisions year-round.

When the sum of your itemized deductions on Schedule A is lower than the standard deduction, you should take the standard deduction. This total is worth checking each year because you may have more deductions in some years and itemizing may make sense.

_____

_____

_____

Because you can control when you pay particular expenses that are eligible for itemizing, you can *shift* or *bunch* more of them into the select years where you have enough deductions to take advantage of itemizing. Suppose, for example, that you're using the standard deduction this year because you don't have many itemized deductions. Late in the year, though, you become certain that you're going to buy a home next year. With mortgage interest and property taxes to write off, you also know that you can itemize next year. If you typically make more charitable contributions in December because of the barrage of solicitations you receive when you're in the giving mood, you may want to write the checks in January rather than in December.

 When you're sure you're not going to have enough deductions in the current year to itemize, try to shift as many expenses as you can into the next tax year.

Real estate deductions

When you buy a home, you can claim two big ongoing expenses of home ownership as deductions on Schedule A: your property taxes and the interest on your mortgage. You're allowed to claim mortgage interest deductions for a primary residence (where you live) and on a second home for mortgage debt totaling $1 million (and a home equity loan of up to $100,000). There's no limit on property tax deductions.

Charitable deductions

You can deduct contributions to charities if you itemize your deductions. Consider the following possibilities:

- Most people know that when they write a check for $50 to their favorite church or college, they can deduct it. *Note:* Make sure you get a receipt for contributions of $250 or more.

- Many taxpayers overlook the fact that you can deduct expenses for work you do with charitable organizations. For example, when you go to a soup kitchen to help prepare and serve meals, you can deduct some of your transportation costs. Keep track of your driving mileage and other commuting expenses.

- You can deduct the fair market value (which can be determined by looking at the price of similar merchandise in thrift stores) of donations of clothing, household appliances, furniture, and other goods to charities. Find out whether organizations such as the Salvation Army, Goodwill, or others are interested in your donation. Just make sure you keep some documentation — write up an itemized list and get it signed by the charity. Take pictures of your more valuable donations.

• You can even donate investments to charity. In fact, donating an appreciated investment gives you a tax deduction for the full market value of the investment and eliminates your need to pay tax on the (unrealized) profit.

Auto registration fees and state insurance

If you don't currently itemize, you may be surprised to discover that your state income taxes can be itemized. When you pay a fee to the state to register and license your car, you can itemize a portion of the expenditure as a deduction (on Schedule A, Line 7, "Personal Property Taxes"). The IRS allows you to deduct the part of the fee that relates to the value of your car. The state organization that collects the fee should be able to tell you what portion of the fee is deductible. (Some states detail on the invoice what portion of the fee is tax deductible.)

Several states have state disability insurance funds. If you pay into these funds (check your W-2), you can deduct your payments as state and local income taxes on Line 5 of Schedule A. You may also claim a deduction on this line for payments you make into your state's unemployment compensation fund.

Deducting miscellaneous expenses

A number of so-called *miscellaneous expenses* are deductible on Schedule A. Most of these expenses relate to your job or career and the management of your finances:

- **Educational expenses:** You may be able to deduct the cost of tuition, books, and travel to and from classes if your education is related to your career. Specifically, you can deduct these expenses if your course work improves your work skills. Courses required by law or your employer to maintain your position are deductible if you pay for them. Continuing education classes for professionals may also be deductible. *Note:* Educational expenses that lead to your moving into a new field or career are not deductible.

- **Job searches and career counseling:** After you obtain your first job, you may deduct legitimate costs related to finding another job within your field. You can even deduct the cost of courses and trips for new job interviews — even if you don't change jobs. And if you hire a career counselor to help you, you can deduct that cost as well.

- **Expenses related to your job that aren't reimbursed:** When you pay for your own subscriptions to trade journals to keep up with your field or buy a new desk and chair to ease back pain, you can deduct these costs. If your job requires you to wear special clothes or a uniform (for example, you're an EMT), you can write off the cost of purchasing and cleaning these clothes, as long as they aren't suitable for wearing outside of work. When you buy a computer for use outside the office at your own expense, you may be able to deduct the cost if the computer is for the convenience of your employer, is a condition of your employment, and is used more than half the time for business. Union dues and membership fees for professional organizations are also deductible.

- **Investment and tax-related expenses:** Investment and tax-advisor fees are deductible when paid from taxable accounts (although fees associated with tax-exempt investments, such as municipal bonds, are not), as are subscription costs for investment-related publications. Accounting fees for preparing your tax return or conducting tax planning during the year are deductible; legal fees related to your taxes are also deductible. If you purchase a home computer to track your investments or prepare your taxes, you can deduct that expense, too.

When you deduct miscellaneous expenses, you get to deduct only the amount that exceeds 2 percent of your AGI (adjusted gross income). *AGI* is your total wage, interest, dividend, and all other income minus retirement account contributions, self-employed health insurance, alimony paid, and losses from investments.

Deducting self-employment expenses

When you're self-employed, you can deduct a multitude of expenses from your income before calculating the tax you owe. If you buy a computer or office furniture, you can deduct those expenses. (Sometimes they need to be gradually deducted, or *depreciated,* over time.) Salaries for your employees, office supplies, rent or mortgage interest for your office space, and phone/communications expenses are also generally deductible.

Many self-employed folks don't take all the deductions they're eligible for. In some cases, people simply aren't aware of the wonderful world of deductions. Others are worried that large deductions will increase the risk of an audit. Spend some time finding out more about tax deductions; you'll be convinced that taking full advantage of your eligible deductions makes sense and saves you money.

The following are common mistakes made by people who are their own bosses:

- **Being an island unto yourself.** When you're self-employed, going it alone is usually a mistake when it comes to taxes. You must educate yourself to make the tax laws work for rather than against you. Hiring tax help is well worth your while. (See "Hiring professional help" later in this chapter for information on hiring tax advisors.)

- **Making administrative tax screw-ups.** As a self-employed individual, you're responsible for the correct and timely filing of all taxes owed on your income and employment taxes on your employees. You need to make estimated tax payments on a quarterly basis. And if you have employees, you also need to withhold taxes from each paycheck they receive and make timely payments to the IRS and the appropriate state authorities. In addition to federal and state income tax, you also need to withhold and send in Social Security and any other state or locally mandated payroll taxes.

  To pay taxes on your income, use Form 1040-ES. This form, along with instructions, can be obtained from the IRS (800-829-3676; www.irs.gov). The form comes complete with an estimated tax worksheet and the four payment coupons you need to send in with your quarterly tax payments. If you want to find the rules for withholding and submitting taxes from employees' paychecks, ask the IRS for Form 941 and Form 940, which is for unemployment insurance. And unless you're lucky enough to live in a state with no income taxes, you need to call for your state's estimated income tax package. Another alternative is to hire a payroll firm to do all this drudgery for you. Scrutinize and negotiate the expenses.

- **Failing to document expenses.** When you pay with cash, following the paper trail for all the money you spent can be hard for you to do (and for the IRS, in the event you're ever audited). At the end of the year, how are you going to remember how much you spent for parking or client meals if you fail to keep a record? How will you survive an IRS audit without proper documentation?

Debit cards are accepted most places and provide a convenient paper trail. (Be careful about getting a debit card in your business's name because some banks don't offer protection against fraudulent use of business debit cards.) Otherwise, you need a record of your daily petty cash purchases. Most pocket calendars or daily organizers include ledgers that allow you to track these small purchases. (Some apps can help with this as well.) If you aren't that organized, at least get receipts for cash transactions and write on each receipt what the purchase was for. Then stash the receipts in a file folder in your desk or keep the receipts in envelopes labeled with the month and year.

- **Failing to fund a retirement plan.** You should be saving money toward retirement anyway, and you can't beat the tax break. People who are self-employed are allowed to save a substantial portion of their net income on an annual basis. (See Chapter 6 for more about retirement planning.)

- **Failing to use numbers to help manage business.** If you're a small-business owner who doesn't track her income, expenses, staff performance, and customer data on a regular basis, your tax return may be the one and only time during the year when you take a financial snapshot of your business. After you go through all the time, trouble, and expense to file your tax return, make sure you reap the rewards of all your work; use those numbers to help analyze and manage your business.

Some bookkeepers and tax preparers can provide you with management information reports on your business from the tax data they compile for you. Just ask. See "Software and websites" later in this chapter for my recommendations.

- **Failing to pay family help.** If your children, spouse, or other relatives help with some aspect of your business, consider paying them for the work. Besides showing them that you value their work, this practice may reduce your family's tax liability. For example, children are usually in a lower tax bracket. By shifting some of your income to family members, you not only cut your tax bill, but can also make them eligible for attractive savings options like IRAs.

Education Tax Breaks

The government offers several tax reduction opportunities for those with educational expenses. Knowing that you don't want to read the dreadful tax code, here's a summary of key provisions you should know about for yourself and your kids if you have them:

- **Student loan interest deduction:** You may take up to a $2,500 deduction for student loan interest that you pay on IRS Form 1040 for college costs as long as your modified adjusted gross income (AGI) is less than or equal to $65,000 for single taxpayers and $130,000 for married couples filing jointly. (*Note:* Your deduction is phased out if your AGI is between $65,000 and $80,000 for single taxpayers and between $130,000 and $160,000 for married couples filing jointly.)

- **Tax-free investment earnings in special accounts:** Money invested in section 529 plans is sheltered from taxation and is not taxed upon withdrawal as long as the money is used to pay for eligible education expenses. Subject to eligibility requirements, 529 plans allow you to sock away $200,000+. Please be aware, however, that funding such accounts may harm your potential financial aid.

- **Tax credits:** The American Opportunity (AO) credit and Lifetime Learning (LL) credit provide tax relief to low- and moderate-income earners facing education costs.

The AO credit may be up to $2,500 per student per year of undergraduate education, while the LL credit may be up to $2,000 per taxpayer. Each student may take only one of these credits per tax year, and they are subject to income limitations. And in a year in which a credit is taken, you may not withdraw money from a 529 plan nor take a tax deduction for your college expenses.

11

Insurance

You may find insurance to be a dreadfully boring topic. Most people associate insurance with disease, death, and disaster and would rather do just about anything other than review their policies or spend money on insurance. But because you won't want to deal with money hassles when you're coping with catastrophes — illness, disability, death, fires, floods, earthquakes, and so on — you should secure insurance well before you need it.

In this chapter, I tell you how to determine what kinds of insurance you need, explain what you can do if you're denied coverage, and give you advice on getting your claims paid.

Basics of Buying Insurance

In this section I boil the subject of insurance down to three fairly simple but powerful concepts that can easily save you money. And while you're saving money, you can still get the quality coverage you need in order to avoid a financial catastrophe.

Insure for the big stuff

The point of insurance is to protect against losses that would be financially catastrophic to you. Some people buy unnecessary policies without knowing it. In the following sections, I tell you how to get the most appropriate insurance coverage for your money. I start off with the biggies that are worth your money, and then I work down to some insurance options that are less worthy of your dollars.

Buy insurance to cover financial catastrophes

You want to insure against what could be a huge financial loss for you or your dependents. The price of insurance isn't cheap, but it's relatively small in comparison to the potential total loss from a financial catastrophe.

The beauty of insurance is that it spreads risks over millions of other people. If your home were to burn to the ground, paying the rebuilding cost out of your own pocket probably would be a financial catastrophe. If you have insurance, the premiums paid by you and all the other homeowners collectively can easily pay the bills.

Think for a moment about what your most valuable assets are. Also consider potential large expenses. Perhaps they include the following:

- **Future income:** During your working years, your most valuable asset is probably your future earnings. If you were disabled and unable to work, what would you live on? Long-term disability insurance exists to help you handle this type of situation. If you have a family that's financially dependent on your earnings, how would your family manage if you died? Life insurance can fill the monetary void left by your death.

- **Business:** If you're a business owner, what would happen if you were sued for hundreds of thousands of dollars or a million dollars or more for negligence in some work that you messed up? Liability insurance can protect you.

- **Health:** In this age of soaring medical costs, you can easily rack up a $100,000 hospital bill in short order. Major medical health insurance helps pay such expenses.

Psychologically, buying insurance coverage for the little things that are more likely to occur is tempting. You don't want to feel like you're wasting your insurance dollars. You want to get some of your money back! You're more *likely* to get into a fender bender with your car or have a package lost in the mail than you are to lose your home to fire or suffer a long-term disability. But if the fender bender costs $500 (which you end up paying out of your pocket because you took my advice to take a high deductible; see the next section) or the postal service loses your package worth $50 or $100, you won't be facing a financial disaster.

On the other hand, if you lose your ability to earn an income because of a disability, or if you're sued for $1 million and you're not insured against such catastrophes, not only will you be extremely unhappy, but you may also face financial ruin.

Take the highest deductible you can afford

Most insurance policies have *deductibles* — the maximum amount you must pay in the event of a loss before your insurance coverage kicks in and begins paying out. On many policies, such as auto and homeowners/renters coverage, most folks opt for a $100 to $250 deductible.

 Here are some benefits of taking a higher deductible:

- **You save premium dollars.** Year in and year out, you can enjoy the lower cost of an insurance policy with a high deductible. You may be able to shave 15 to 20 percent off the cost of your policy. Suppose, for example, that you can reduce the cost of your policy by $150 per year by raising your deductible from $250 to $1,000. That $750 worth of coverage is costing you $150 per year. Thus, you'd need to have a claim of $1,000 or more every five years — highly unlikely — to come out ahead. If you're that accident-prone, guess what? The insurance company will raise your premiums.

- **You don't have the hassles of filing small claims.** If you have a $300 loss on a policy with a $100 deductible, you need to file a claim to get your $200 (the amount you're covered for after your deductible). Filing an insurance claim can be an aggravating experience that takes hours of time. In some cases, you may even have your claim denied after jumping through all the necessary hoops. Getting your due may require prolonged haggling.

When you have low deductibles, you may file more claims (although this doesn't necessarily mean that you'll get more money). After filing more claims, you may be "rewarded" with higher premiums — in addition to the headache you get from preparing all those blasted forms! Filing more claims may even cause cancellation of your coverage.

Avoid small-potato policies

A good insurance policy can seem expensive. A policy that doesn't cost much, on the other hand, can fool you into thinking that you're getting something for next to nothing. Policies that cost little also cover little — they're priced low because they don't cover large potential losses.

Following are examples of common "small-potato" insurance policies that are generally a waste of your hard-earned

_____

_____

_____

dollars. These policies aren't worth the cost relative to the small potential benefit. On average, insurance companies pay out just 60 cents in benefits on every dollar collected. Many of the following policies pay back even less — around 20 cents in benefits (claims) for every insurance premium dollar spent:

- **Extended warranty and repair plans:** Extended warranty and repair plans are expensive and unnecessary short-term insurance policies. Product manufacturers' warranties typically cover any problems that occur in the first year or even several years. After that, paying for a repair out of your own pocket isn't a financial catastrophe.

- **Home warranty plans:** If your real estate agent or the seller of a home wants to pay the cost of a home warranty plan for you, turning down the offer would be ungracious. But don't buy this type of plan for yourself. In addition to requiring some sort of fee (around $50 to $100), home warranty plans limit how much they'll pay for problems.

- **Dental insurance:** If your employer pays for dental insurance, you could take advantage of it. But don't pay for this coverage on your own. Dental insurance generally covers a couple of teeth cleanings each year and limits payments for more expensive work.

- **Credit life and credit disability policies:** Credit life policies pay a small benefit if you die with an outstanding loan. Credit disability policies pay a small monthly income in the event of a disability. Banks and their credit card divisions usually sell these policies. Some companies sell insurance to pay off your credit card bill in the event of your death or disability, or to cover minimum monthly payments for a temporary period during specified life transition events (such as loss of a job, divorce, and so on).

  If you're in poor health and you can buy these insurance policies without a medical evaluation, you may represent an exception to the "don't buy it" rule. In this case, these policies may be the only ones to which you have access — another reason these policies are expensive. The people in good health are paying for the people with poor health who can enroll without a medical examination and who undoubtedly file more claims.

- **Daily hospitalization insurance:** Hospitalization insurance policies that pay a certain amount per day,

_____

_____

_____

such as $100, prey on people's fears of running up big hospital bills. Healthcare is expensive — there's no doubt about that.

What you really need is a comprehensive (major medical) health insurance policy. One day in the hospital can lead to thousands of dollars in charges, so that $100-per-day policy may pay for less than an hour of your 24-hour day. Daily hospitalization policies don't cover the big-ticket expenses. If you lack a comprehensive health insurance policy, make sure you get one.

- **Little stuff riders:** Many policies that are worth buying, such as auto and disability insurance, can have all sorts of riders added on. These *riders* are extra bells and whistles that insurance agents and companies like to sell because of the high profit margin they provide (for *them*). On auto insurance policies, for example, you can buy a rider for a few bucks per year that pays you $25 each time your car needs to be towed. Having your vehicle towed isn't going to bankrupt you, so it isn't worth insuring against.

Buy broad coverage

Purchasing coverage that's too narrow is another major mistake people make when buying insurance. Such policies often seem like cheap ways to put your fears to rest. For example, instead of buying life insurance, some folks buy flight insurance when they purchase their airline tickets. They seem to worry more about their mortality when getting on an airplane than they do when getting into a car. If they die on the flight, their beneficiaries collect. But should they die the next day in an auto accident or get some dreaded disease — which is statistically far more likely than going down in a jumbo jet — the beneficiaries get nothing from flight insurance. Buy life insurance (broad coverage to protect your loved ones financially in the event of your death no matter how you die), not flight insurance (narrow coverage).

The medical equivalent of flight insurance is cancer insurance. Older people, who are fearful of having their life savings depleted by a long battle with this dreaded disease, are easy prey for this narrow insurance. If you get cancer, cancer insurance pays the bills. But what if you get heart disease, diabetes, or some other disease? Cancer insurance won't pay these costs. Purchase major medical coverage, not cancer insurance.

Recognize fears

Fears, such as getting cancer, are natural and inescapable. Although you may not have control over the emotions that your fears invoke, you must often ignore those emotions in order to make rational insurance decisions. In other words, getting shaky in the knees and sweaty in the palms when boarding an airplane is okay, but letting your fear of flying cause you to make poor insurance decisions is not okay, especially when those decisions affect the financial security of your loved ones.

Prepare for natural disasters

You'll find it nearly impossible to get coverage that includes every possibility of catastrophe. For example, when purchasing homeowners coverage, you find that losses from floods and earthquakes are excluded. You can secure such coverage in separate policies, which you should do if you live in an area subject to such risks. Many people don't understand these risks, and insurers don't always educate customers about such gaping holes in their policies.

Shop around and buy direct

Whether you're looking at auto, home, life, disability, or other types of coverage, some companies may charge double or triple the rates that other companies charge for the same coverage. Insurers that charge the higher rates may not be better about paying claims, however. You may even end up with the worst of both possible worlds — high prices *and* lousy service.

Most insurance is sold through agents and brokers who earn commissions based on what they sell. The commissions, of course, can bias what they recommend.

Not surprisingly, policies that pay agents the biggest commissions also tend to be more costly. In fact, insurance companies compete for the attention of agents by offering bigger commissions.

Besides the attraction of policies that pay higher commissions, agents also get hooked, financially speaking, on companies whose policies they sell frequently. After an agent sells a certain amount of a company's insurance policies, she is rewarded with bigger commission percentages (and other perks) on any future sales.

Shopping around is a challenge not only because most insurance is sold by agents working on commission, but also because insurers set their rates in mysterious ways. Every company has a different way of analyzing how much of a risk you are; one company may offer low rates to me but not to you, and vice versa.

Despite the obstacles, several strategies exist for obtaining low-cost, high-quality policies. The following sections offer smart ways to shop for insurance.

Employer and other group plans

When you buy insurance as part of a larger group, you generally get a lower price because of the purchasing power of the group. Most of the health and disability policies that you can access through your employer are less costly than equivalent coverage you can buy on your own.

Likewise, many occupations have professional associations through which you may be able to obtain lower-cost policies. Not all associations offer better deals on insurance — compare their policy features and costs with other options.

Life insurance is an exception to the rule that states that group policies offer better value than individual policies. Group life insurance plans usually aren't cheaper than the best life insurance policies that you can buy individually. However,

_____

_____

_____

group policies may have the attraction of convenience (ease of enrollment and avoidance of lengthy sales pitches from life insurance salespeople). Group life insurance policies that allow you to enroll without a medical evaluation are usually more expensive because such plans attract more people with health problems who can't get coverage on their own. If you're in good health, you should definitely shop around for life insurance.

Insurance agents who want to sell you an individual policy can come up with 101 reasons why buying from them is preferable to buying through your employer or some other group. In most cases, agents' arguments for buying an individual policy from them include self-serving hype.

One valid issue that agents raise is that if you leave your job, you'll lose your group coverage. Sometimes that may be true. For example, if you know you're going to be leaving your job to become self-employed, securing an individual disability policy before you leave your job makes sense. However, your employer's health insurer may allow you to buy an individual policy when you leave.

_____

_____

_____

Buying insurance without paying sales commissions

Buying policies from the increasing number of companies that are selling their policies directly to the public without the insurance agent and the agent's commission is your best bet for getting a good insurance value.

Annuities, investment/insurance products traditionally sold through insurance agents, are also now available directly to the customer without commission. Simply contact some of the leading no-load mutual fund companies.

Insurance Problems

When you seek out insurance or have insurance policies, sooner or later you're bound to hit a roadblock. Although insurance problems can be among the more frustrating in life, in the following sections, I explain how to successfully deal with the more common obstacles.

_____

_____

_____

If you're denied coverage

Just as you can be turned down when you apply for a loan, you can also be turned down when applying for insurance. With life or disability insurance, a company may reject you if you have an existing medical problem (a preexisting condition) and are therefore more likely to file a claim. When it comes to insuring assets such as a home, you may have difficulty getting coverage if the property is deemed to be in a high-risk area.

 Here are some strategies to employ if you're denied coverage:

- **Ask the insurer why you were denied.** Perhaps the company made a mistake or misinterpreted some information in your application. If you're denied coverage because of a medical condition, find out what information the company has on you and determine whether it's accurate.

- **Request a copy of your medical information file.** Just as you have a credit report file that details your use (and misuse) of credit, you also have a medical information report. Once per year, you can request a free copy of your medical information file (which typically highlights only the more significant problems over the past seven years, not your entire medical file or history) by calling 866-692-6901 or visiting the website at www.mib.com (click on the link on the homepage for Consumers). If you find a mistake on your report, you have the right to request that it be fixed. However, the burden is on you to prove that the information in your file is incorrect. Proving that your file contains errors can be a major hassle — you may even need to contact physicians you saw in the past because their medical records may be the source of the incorrect information.

- **Shop other companies.** Just because one company denies you coverage (for example, with disability or life insurance) doesn't mean all insurance companies will do the same. Some insurers better understand certain medical conditions and are more comfortable accepting applicants with those conditions. While most insurers charge higher rates to people with blemished medical histories than they do to people with perfect health records, some companies penalize them less than others. An agent who sells policies from multiple insurers, called an *independent agent*, can be helpful because she can shop among a number of different companies.

- **Find out about state high-risk pools.** Before the passage of the Affordable Care Act (also known as Obamacare), most states acted as the insurer of last resort and provided basic insurance, through high-risk pools, for those who couldn't get it from insurance companies. Because health insurers can no longer deny coverage due to preexisting health problems, numerous states have ended their high-risk pools. The Health Insurance Resource Center website at www.healthinsurance.org/obamacare/risk-pools/ provides links to all state health coverage high-risk pool websites still offering such coverage. Alternatively, you can check with your state department of insurance (search the Internet using your state's name and "state department of insurance") for high-risk pools for other types of insurance, such as property coverage.

- **Check for coverage availability before you buy.** If you're considering buying a home, for example, and you can't get coverage, the insurance companies are trying to tell you something. What they're effectively saying is, "We think that property is so high-risk, we're not willing to insure it even if you pay a high premium."

Getting your due on claims

In the event that you suffer a loss and file an insurance claim, you naturally hope that your insurance company will cheerfully and expeditiously pay your claims. Given all the money that you shelled out for coverage and all the hoops you jumped through to get approved for coverage in the first place, that's a reasonable expectation.

Insurance companies may refuse to pay you what you think they owe you for many reasons, however. In some cases, your claim may not be covered under the terms of the policy. At a minimum, the insurer wants documentation and proof of your loss. Other people have been known to cheat, so insurers won't simply take your word, no matter how honest and ethical you are.

Some insurers view paying claims as an adversarial situation and take a "negotiate tough" stance. Thinking that all insurance companies are going to pay you a fair and reasonable amount even if you don't make your voice heard is a mistake.

The tips I discuss in this section can help you ensure that you get paid what your policy entitles you to.

Document your assets and case

When you're insuring assets, such as your home and its contents, having a record of what you own can be helpful if you need to file a claim. If you keep records of valuables and can document their cost, you should be in good shape. A video is the most efficient record for documenting your assets, but a handwritten list detailing your possessions works, too. Just remember to keep this record someplace away from your home; if your home burns to the ground, you'll lose your documentation.

If you're robbed or are the victim of an accident, get the names, addresses, and phone numbers of witnesses. Take pictures of property damage and solicit estimates for the cost of repairing or replacing whatever has been lost or damaged. File police reports when appropriate, if for no other reason than to bolster your documentation for the insurance claim.

_____

_____

_____

Prepare your case

Filing a claim should be viewed the same way as preparing for a court trial or an IRS audit. Any information you provide verbally or in writing can and will be used against you to deny your claim. First, you should understand whether your policy covers your claim (this is why getting the broadest possible coverage helps). The only way to find out whether the policy covers your claim is to read it. Policies are hard to read because they use legal language in non-user-friendly ways.

A possible alternative to reading your policy is to call the claims department and, *without* providing your name (and using caller ID blocking on your phone), ask a representative whether a particular loss (such as the one that you just suffered) is covered under its policy. You have no need to lie to the company, but you don't have to tell the representative who you are and that you're about to file a claim, either. Your call is so you can understand what your policy covers. However, some companies aren't willing to provide detailed information unless a specific case is cited.

_____

_____

_____

After you initiate the claims process, keep records of all conversations and copies of all the documents you give to the insurer's claims department. If you have problems down the road, this "evidence" may bail you out.

For property damage, get a couple of reputable contractors' estimates. Demonstrate to the insurance company that you're trying to shop for a low price, but don't agree to use a low-cost contractor without knowing that she can do quality work.

Approach your claim as a negotiation

To get what you're owed on an insurance claim, you must approach most claims' filings for what they are — a negotiation with a party that's often uncooperative. And the bigger the claim, the more your insurer will play the part of adversary.

Be persistent

When you take an insurance company's first offer and don't fight for what you're due, you may be leaving a lot of money on the table.

_____

_____

_____

Enlisting support

If you're doing your homework and you're not making progress with the insurer's adjuster, ask to speak with supervisors and managers.

The agent who sold you the policy may be helpful in preparing and filing the claim. A good agent can help increase your chances of getting paid — and getting paid sooner. If you're having difficulty with a claim for a policy obtained through your employer or other group, speak with the benefits department or a person responsible for interacting with the insurer. These folks have a lot of clout because the agent and/or insurer doesn't want to lose the entire account.

If you're having problems getting a fair settlement from the insurer of a policy you bought on your own, try contacting the state department of insurance. You can find the phone number online or possibly in your insurance policy.

Hiring a public adjuster who, for a percentage of the payment (typically 5 to 10 percent), can negotiate with insurers on your behalf is another option.

_____

_____

_____

When all else fails and you have a major claim at stake, try contacting an attorney who specializes in insurance matters. You can find these specialists by entering "Attorneys — Insurance Law" and your city into a search engine. Expect to pay $100+ per hour. Look for a lawyer who's willing to negotiate on your behalf, help draft letters, and perform other necessary tasks on an hourly basis without filing a lawsuit. Your state department of insurance, the local bar association, or other legal, accounting, or financial practitioners also may be able to refer you to someone.

_____

_____

_____

12

Technology and Your Money

Although a computer and, to a lesser extent, a smartphone may be able to assist you with your personal finances, they simply represent a couple of many tools. Computers are best for performing routine tasks (such as processing lots of bills or performing many calculations) quickly and for aiding you with research.

This chapter gives you an overview of how to use technology and software with your finances. I tell you how to use this technology to pay your bills, prepare taxes, and plan for retirement, and I suggest the best software, websites, and apps.

Digital Pros and Cons

You can use software and websites to manage your personal finance information through your computer.

Benefits of financial software

Although the number of personal finance software packages, apps, and websites is large and growing, quality is lagging behind quantity, especially among the free Internet sites. The best programs can

- Guide you to better organization and management of your personal finances
- Help you complete mundane tasks or complex calculations quickly and easily and provide basic advice in unfamiliar territory
- Make you feel in control of your financial life

Mediocre and bad software, on the other hand, can make you feel stupid or, at the very least, make you want to scream. Lousy packages usually end up in the software graveyard.

Having reviewed many of the packages available, I can assure you that if you're having a hard time with some of the programs out there (and sometimes even with the more useful programs), you're not at fault. Too many packages assume that you already know things such as your tax rate, your mortgage options, and the difference between stock and bond mutual funds. Much of what's out there is too technically oriented and isn't user-friendly. Some of it is even flawed in its financial accuracy.

A good software package, like a good tax or financial advisor, helps you better manage your finances. It simply and concisely explains financial terminology, and it helps you make decisions by offering choices and recommendations, allowing you to "play" with alternatives before following a particular course of action. With increasing regularity, financial software packages are being designed to perform more than one task or to address more than one area of personal finances. But no software package covers the whole range of issues in your financial life.

Online perils

Like the information you receive from any medium, you have to sift out the good from the bad when you surf the Internet. If you blindly navigate the Internet and naively think that what's out there is useful "information," "research," or "objective advice," you're in for a rude awakening.

Most personal finance sites on the Internet are free, which means that these sites are basically advertising or are dominated and driven by advertising. If you're looking for material written by unbiased experts or writers, finding it on the web may seem like searching for the proverbial needle in the haystack because the vast majority of what's online is biased and uninformed.

Bias

A report on the Internet published by a leading investment banking firm provides a list of the "coolest finance" sites. On the list is the website of a major bank. If cool can be used to describe a well-organized and graphically pleasing website, then I guess the bank's site is cool.

However, if you're looking for sound information and advice, the bank's site is decidedly "uncool." It steers you in a financial direction that benefits the bank and not you. For example, in the real estate section, users are asked to plug in their gross monthly income and down payment. The information is then used to spit out the supposed amount that users can "afford" to spend on a home. No mention is given to the other financial goals and concerns — such as saving for retirement — that affect one's ability to spend a particular amount of money on a home.

"Sponsored" content

Sponsored content, a euphemism for advertising under the guise of editorial content (known in the print media as *advertorials*), is another big problem to watch out for on websites. You may find a disclaimer or note, which is often buried in small print in an obscure part of the website, saying that an article is sponsored by (in other words, paid advertising by) the "author."

A mutual fund "education" site, for example, states that its "primary purpose is to provide viewers with an independent guide that contains information and articles they can't get anywhere else." The content of the site suggests otherwise. In the "Expert's Corner" section of the site, material is reprinted from a newsletter that advocates frequent trading in and out of mutual funds to try and guess and time market moves. Turns out that the article is "sponsored by the featured expert": In other words, it's a paid advertisement.

Even more troubling is the increasing number of websites that fail to disclose that their "content" comes from advertisers. Print publications generally have a tradition of disclosing when an article is paid advertising, but in the Wild West online, many sites fail to make this simple and vital disclosure.

Increasingly, companies are paying websites outright to simply mention and praise their products; doing so is sleazy even if it's disclosed, but to do so without disclosure is unethical. Also beware of links to recommended product and service providers — more often than not, the referring website gets paid an affiliate fee. Look for sites that post policies against receiving such referral fees from companies whose products and services they recommend.

Biased financial planning advice

Skip the financial planning advice offered by financial service companies that are out to sell you something. Such companies can't take the necessary objective, holistic view required to render useful advice.

For example, on one major investment company's website, you find a good deal of material on the firm's mutual funds. The site's college planning advice is off the mark because it urges parents to put money in a custodial account in the child's name. Ignored is the fact that doing so will undermine your child's ability to qualify for financial aid, that your child will have control of the money at either age 18 or 21 depending on your state, and that you're likely better off funding your employer's retirement plan. If you did that, though, you couldn't set up a college savings-plan account at the fund company.

Short-term thinking

Many financial websites provide real-time stock quotes as a hook to a site that is cluttered with advertising. My experience working with individual investors is that the more short term they think, the worse they do. And checking your portfolio during the trading day certainly promotes short-term thinking.

Another way that sites create an addictive environment for you to return to multiple times daily is to constantly provide news and other rapidly changing content. Do you really need "Breaking News" updates that gasoline prices jumped 19 cents per gallon over the past two weeks?

Also, beware of tips offered around the electronic water cooler — comment sections. As in the real world, chatting with strangers and exchanging ideas are sometimes fine. However, if you don't know the identity and competence of commenters, why would you follow their financial advice or stock tips? Getting ideas from various sources is okay, but educate yourself and do your homework before making personal financial decisions.

If you want to best manage your personal finances and find out more, remember that the old expression "You get what you pay for" contains a grain of truth. Free information on the Internet, especially information provided by companies in the financial services industry, is largely self-serving. Stick with information providers who have proven themselves offline or who don't have anything to sell except objective information and advice.

Accomplishing Money Tasks on Your Digital Device

In the remainder of this chapter, I detail important personal financial tasks that your computer, tablet, or smartphone can assist you with. I also provide my recommendations for the best software and websites to help you accomplish these chores.

Paying your bills and tracking your money

Plenty of folks have trouble saving money and reducing their spending. Thus, it's no surprise that in the crowded universe of free websites, plenty are devoted to supposedly helping you reduce your spending. More of these websites and apps keep springing up, but among those you may have heard of and stumbled upon are Geezeo, Mint, Mvelopes, Wally, and Yodlee.

I've kicked the tires and checked out these sites and frankly have mixed to negative feelings about them. The biggest problems I have with these sites are that they're loaded with advertising and/or have *affiliate relationships* with companies. What does this mean? The site gets paid if you click on a link to one of its recommended service providers and buy what it's selling.

Also, be forewarned that after registering you as a site user, the first thing most of these sites want you to do is connect directly to your financial institutions (banks, brokerages, investment companies) and download your investment account and spending data. If your instincts tell you this might not be a good idea, you should trust your instincts. Yes, there are security concerns, but those pale in comparison to privacy concerns and concerns about the endless pitching to you of products and services.

Another problem I have with these websites is the simplistic calculators they offer. One that purported to help with retirement planning didn't allow users to choose a retirement age younger than 62 and had no provisions for part-time work. When it asked about your assets, it made no distinction between equity in your home and financial assets (stocks, bonds, mutual funds, and so on).

Quicken is a good software program that helps with expense tracking and bill paying. In addition to offering printed checks and electronic bill payment, Quicken is a financial organizer. The program allows you to list your investments and other assets, along with your loans and other financial liabilities. Quicken automates the process of paying your bills, and it can track your check writing and prepare reports that detail your spending by category so you can find the fat in your budget. (For a complete discussion on how to track your spending, see Chapter 4.)

You can avoid dealing with paper checks — written or printed — by signing up for *online bill payment*. With such services, you save on checks, stamps, and envelopes. These services are available to anyone with a checking account through an increasing number of banks, credit unions, and brokerage firms, as well as through Quicken. Another option is to sign up through CheckFree's website: www.mycheckfree.com.

_____

_____

_____

Planning for retirement

Good retirement planning software and online tools can help you plan for retirement by crunching the numbers for you. But they can also teach you how particular changes — such as your investment returns, the rate of inflation, or your savings rate — can affect when and in what style you can retire. The biggest time-saving aspect of retirement planning software and websites is that they let you more quickly play with and see the consequences of changing the assumptions.

The following investment companies are good sources for some high-quality, low-cost retirement-planning tools:

- **T. Rowe Price's** website (www.troweprice.com) has several tools that can help you determine where you stand in terms of reaching a given retirement goal. T. Rowe Price (800-225-5132) also offers some excellent workbooklets for helping you plan for retirement. Expect some marketing of T. Rowe Price's mutual funds in its booklets and software.

_____

_____

_____

- **Vanguard's** website (www.vanguard.com) can help with figuring savings goals to reach retirement goals as well as with managing your budget and assets in retirement.

Preparing your taxes

Good, properly used tax preparation software can save you time and money. The best programs "interview" you to gather the necessary information and select the appropriate forms based on your responses. Of course, you're still the one responsible for locating all the information needed to complete your return. More-experienced taxpayers can bypass the interview and jump directly to the forms they know they need to complete. These programs also help flag overlooked deductions and identify other tax-reducing strategies.

TurboTax and H&R Block Tax Software are among the better tax-preparation programs I've reviewed.

In addition to the federal tax packages, tax preparation programs are available for state income taxes, too. Many state tax forms are fairly easy to complete because they're based on information from your federal form. If your state tax forms are based on your federal form, you may want to skip buying the state income-tax preparation packages and prepare your state return by hand.

 If you're mainly looking for tax forms, you can get them at no charge in tax preparation books or through the IRS's website (www.irs.gov).

_____

_____

_____

About the Author

Eric Tyson, MBA, first became interested in money more than three decades ago. After his father was laid off during a recession and received some retirement money from his employer, Eric worked with his dad to make investing decisions with the money. A couple of years later, Eric won his high school's science fair with a project on what influences the stock market.

After toiling away for a number of years as a management consultant to Fortune 500 financial service firms, Eric finally figured out how to pursue his dream. He took his inside knowledge of the banking, investment, and insurance industries and committed himself to making personal financial management accessible to all.

Today, Eric is an internationally acclaimed and best-selling personal finance book author, syndicated columnist, and speaker. He has worked with and taught people from all financial situations, so he knows the financial concerns and questions of real folks just like you. Despite being handicapped by an MBA from the Stanford Graduate School of Business and a BS in economics and biology from Yale University, Eric remains a master of "keeping it simple."

Eric's website is www.erictyson.com.